Culinary Arts Institute

NUTRITION
COOKBOOK

Featured in cover photo:
The Basic Four, 13-14

NUTRITION

NUTRITION COOKBOOK

The Culinary Arts Institute Staff:
Helen Geist: Director
Sherrill Corley: Editor • Helen Lehman: Assistant Editor
Edward Finnegan: Executive Editor • Charles Bozett: Art Director
Ethel La Roche: Editorial Assistant • Ivanka Simatic: Recipe Tester
Malinda Miller: Copy Editor • John Mahalek: Art Assembly

Book designed and coordinated by Charles Bozett and Laurel DiGangi

Illustrations by Seymour Fleishman

Cover photo: Zdenek Pivecka

Adventures in Cooking SERIES

COOKBOOK

Culinary Arts Institute

1975 Hawthorne, Melrose Park, Illinois, 60160

PHOTO ACKNOWLEDGMENTS

Alaska King Crab; Fleischmann's Yeast;
Halibut Association of North America;
National Broiler Council; National Live Stock and Meat Board;
Pacific Bartlett Growers, Inc.; Rice Council;
United Fresh Fruit and Vegetable Association

Contents

Nutrition Know-How

Nutrition is one of the most important factors in the achievement of good health. Good health does not only mean being free from disease. Good nutrition helps us look better, feel better, think better, work better, and live longer. Nutrition is the process of eating and using food. We need to understand the body's nutrient requirements, learn how to select foods that will fulfill those requirements, and develop good eating patterns that provide pleasurable and healthful meals.

Unfortunately, our eating habits (the foods we eat, how we get them, and how we eat meals) are often careless. No longer do we eat at the set hours of eight, twelve, and six. Lifestyles have changed, and although many of us eat three meals a day, those meals may be rushed, and the in-between hours are filled with snacks. We may, in fact, eat six or seven "meals" a day, giving little thought to variety or nourishment.

Many people interested in good health are too often swayed by the words of self-styled food experts who guarantee us good health if we follow their special diets. No single food, method, or diet can fulfill the body's nutritional needs. Indeed, the effects of these diet fads are sometimes disastrous.

Our philosophy of good nutrition, endorsed by medical authorities, is simple: a variety of foods from common sources, eaten in moderation. Proper nourishment does not depend upon following a rigid dietary regimen—there is a wide world of foods and food combinations to choose from.

This book will give you the know-how to plan, purchase, store, and prepare a variety of good, nourishing foods. And it will provide you with recipes designed to combine and take advantage of the nutritional value of a variety of foods.

THE INDIVIDUAL NUTRIENTS

Nutrients are the individual substances that combine to make foods and to supply us with all we need to move, to grow, to live. They are usually grouped in five categories: proteins, carbohydrates, fats, vitamins, and minerals. Another substance important to nutrition is water. Sections on each of these nutrients follow.

PROTEIN

Proteins are the body builders and body maintainers. They help develop muscles and create a feeling of fitness. In addition, proteins help make hemoglobin, the blood protein that delivers oxygen to and removes carbon dioxide from cells. Proteins are part of hormones (which regulate growth and body functions), of enzymes (which produce chemical changes in the body), and of genes (which determine the development of hereditary characteristics). Proteins help form antibodies to fight infections, and they are an energy source.

Amino acids, twenty-two of them, are the building blocks of protein. Eight of them must be obtained from food eaten daily.

Proteins are called high-quality (adequate) if they supply all the eight essential amino acids in proper amounts. Beef, lamb, pork, poultry, fish, shellfish, eggs, and milk are high-quality sources.

PICK A PROTEIN

Food Group	Portion	Protein Grams	Food Group	Portion	Protein Grams
Milk			Pork, cooked, lean to medium-fat	3 oz.	18
Milk			Salmon, pink, canned	3 oz.	17
Whole	1 cup	9	Sardines, canned, drained	3 oz.	20
2% (nonfat milk solids added)	1 cup	10	Shrimps, canned	3 oz.	21
Skim	1 cup	9	Tuna, canned, drained	3 oz.	24
Buttermilk	1 cup	9	Veal, cooked, lean to medium-fat	3 oz.	23
Nonfat dry, reconstituted	1 cup	8	**Fruit and Vegetable**		
Cheese			Apricots, dried	½ cup	4
American	1 slice (1 oz.)	7	Beans, lima	½ cup	6
Blue or Roquefort	¼ cup (1 oz.)	6	Brussels sprouts	½ cup	4
Camembert	1 wedge (1⅓ oz.)	7	Corn	½ cup	3
Cheddar	1 slice (1 oz.)	7	Peas, green	½ cup	4
Cottage, creamed	½ cup	16	Potato	1 medium	3
Cream cheese	3 oz.	7	**Bread and Cereal**		
Swiss	1 slice (1 oz.)	8	Bagel	1	6
Ice cream, vanilla	½ cup	3	Bread		
Yogurt, plain	1 cup	8	Rye	2 slices	4
Meat			White	2 slices	4
Bacon, crisp	2 slices	5	Whole wheat	2 slices	6
Beans, baked, with pork	1 cup (8 oz.)	16	Cereal, cooked	1 cup	4
Beans, dried, cooked	1 cup (5 oz.)	14	Corn muffin, plain	1	3
Beef, cooked, lean to medium-fat	3 oz.	23	Macaroni, cooked	1 cup	6
Bologna or lunch meat	2 slices (1 oz.)	3	Noodles, cooked	1 cup	7
Chicken, broiled, boneless	3 oz.	20	Pancakes (4-inch)	2	4
Clams, canned, meat and liquid	3 oz.	7	Rice, cooked	1 cup	4
Clams, raw meat	3 oz.	11	Waffle (7-inch)	1	7
Crabmeat, canned	3 oz.	15	**Miscellaneous**		
Egg	1 large	6	Cream, dairy sour	1 cup	7
Fish, breaded, fried	3 oz.	17	Custard, baked	½ cup	7
Frankfurter	1 (2 oz.)	7	Danish pastry	1	5
Ham	1 slice (1 oz.)	6	Eclair, chocolate	1	8
Lamb, cooked, lean to medium-fat	3 oz.	21	Gelatin dessert	1 cup	4
Liver, beef, fried	3 oz.	22	Pie	⅙ of 9-inch	
Nuts, shelled, roasted	¼ cup (1 oz.)	6	Custard		9
Oysters, raw meat	3 oz.	7	Fruit		3
Peanut butter	2 tablespoons	8	Pecan		7
Pea soup, canned	1 cup (8 oz.)	9	Pizza	⅛ of 14-inch	7
Peas, split, dried, cooked	1 cup	20	Pudding		
			Chocolate	½ cup	4
			Rice, with raisins	½ cup	5
			Vanilla	½ cup	5

A low-quality protein has too little of some of the eight essential amino acids. These include vegetables such as lentils and the legumes. Vegetable protein sources are called meat substitutes. Cereal grains, some fruits, and several other vegetables also contain some protein. They are usually cheap, plentiful, and filling.

Many vegetarians manage their protein needs by carefully balancing vegetable proteins with each other to provide the eight amino acids in proper amounts. Most people, however, opt for the simple protein insurance policy of eating both vegetable and animal proteins.

Because our bodies cannot store amino acids, we need small amounts of protein daily, preferably at each meal. Nutritionists recommend that protein comprise about 15 percent of a day's calorie intake, or one gram of protein for each kilogram of body weight (0.424 grams per pound of body weight). This is forty-six grams for the average woman and fifty-six for the average man. Most adults in the United States regularly consume eighty to ninety grams per day. The extra protein is simply used for energy.

One typical diet mistake is that we often ignore the calorie cost of high-protein foods, erroneously assuming that protein is "thinning." Six ounces of sirloin steak will indeed give you forty grams of protein—at a cost of 660 calories. Planning, selection, and moderation are all important when it comes to putting protein in your meals.

CARBOHYDRATES

The belief that carbohydrates are fattening is partially true, but it can be dangerous. Carbohydrates provide energy and process fatty acids in the body. Furthermore, the grain products, fruits, and vegetables that supply our bodies with carbohydrates also provide many essential vitamins and minerals.

Carbohydrates are organic substances made up of carbon, hydrogen, and oxygen. They include simple sugars (monosaccharides) such as glucose, fructose, and galactose; disaccharides, such as table sugar; and complex carbohydrates (starches and cellulose).

Starches and sugars are two of our major energy sources. Sugars are the simplest carbohydrates, and whatever their form, are all basically the same. Starches are bunches of simple sugars chemically combined. Because they are more complex than sugars, they digest slightly more slowly.

Generally, research indicates that we might be better off eating less sugar and getting our carbohydrates from other foods that also supply vitamins and minerals. Some of them add protein, too.

Eliminating carbohydrates from the diet is downright dangerous. Both carbohydrates and fats together are necessary for proper fuel chemistry. Without carbohydrates, fats are not completely broken down, and substances called ketones are formed. If ketones are allowed to build up, they become poisonous and produce a serious and sometimes fatal condition called ketosis.

Carbohydrates comprise about 45 to 50 percent of the calories in the average American diet. Carbohydrate intake can go as high as 55 percent of calories in a healthful diet. Unfortunately, in more affluent societies, carbohydrates tend to be slighted and fat intake increased. Many Americans may consume more than 50 percent of their daily calorie intake in the form of fat. Nutrition experts recommend limiting fat in the diet to 30 to 35 percent. Wise food selection and moderation are essential in balancing fat and carbohydrate intake.

FATS

Fat is probably the most controversial item in our diet. How much and what kind of fat do we need? You've heard fats described as saturated, unsaturated, polyunsaturated, and hydrogenated. What do these terms mean?

Fats are a concentrated source of energy. Gram for gram, ounce for ounce, fats supply more than twice as much energy (or calories) as proteins or carbohydrates.

They carry vitamins A, D, E, and K; make up a part of the cell structure; protect our vital organs; provide energy for proteins; and insulate the body. We all need some fat in our diets.

Fats are classified according to the amount of certain kinds of fatty acids they contain. *Saturated* fatty acids are of animal origin. They include the fat on and in meat, butterfat from and in whole milk products, and lard. *Unsaturated* and *polyunsaturated* fatty acids are found in liquid oils from plant sources: corn, cottonseed, safflower, sesame, soy, or wheat germ. *Hydrogenated* fatty acids are unsaturated or polyunsaturated fatty acids to which hydrogen has been added.

Unless otherwise instructed by your physician, follow the advice of the United States Department of Agriculture: "In choosing daily meals, it is well to keep the total amount of fat at a moderate level and to include some foods that contain polyunsaturated fats."

CHOLESTEROL

Cholesterol is an organic substance. In the human body, cholesterol is an important part of nerve tissue (and therefore of the brain) and of digestive juices, and it plays a significant role in the formation of steroid hormones. Although our bodies produce cholesterol, the cholesterol level in the blood is dependent to an extent on the foods we eat. Cholesterol is found in foods of animal origin, especially organ meats, shellfish, egg yolks, and animal fats. Fruits, vegetables, cereal grains, legumes, nuts, oil, or anything else coming from plants have no cholesterol content.

In spite of cholesterol's usefulness in our bodies, too much cholesterol in the blood may be dangerous. The question posed by medical authorities is whether lowering the level of cholesterol in the blood will diminish the possibility of heart disease and related conditions. The American Heart Association believes that a diet low in cholesterol and low in saturated fats can decrease the risk of heart disease. If you have questions concerning your cholesterol level, consult your doctor.

VITAMINS

It is only within the last fifty years that man has started to learn about vitamins. They are essential to life and well-being. Moreover, we cannot manufacture most vitamins in our bodies. Fortunately, vitamins are vitamins, whatever their source—natural or synthetic.

Lack of vitamins causes deficiency diseases. Each of the better-known vitamins is related to an equally well-known disease. The remarkable thing about these diseases is that the cure is usually simple and immediately effective. Start eating foods that have the proper amount of the vitamin you need and it won't be long before you are well. A word of warning here—vitamin deficiency diseases *can* be cured by certain foods. Other diseases *cannot* be cured by certain foods.

About a dozen or so major vitamins have been identified. They are available from foods in your neighborhood grocery store.

Vitamin pills and supplements are not necessary additions to a varied, balanced diet. If you want extra insurance, check with your doctor and take a vitamin pill containing United States Recommended Daily Allowances (U.S. RDA) and *no more than those recommended amounts.* Taking massive doses of vitamins or megavitamins is unwise and dangerous. Few people realize that excesses of some vitamins can be poisonous and even fatal. Vitamin overdose is almost always due to abuse of vitamin supplements. Therapeutic vitamin intake must be supervised by a physician.

Vitamin C (Ascorbic Acid)

Vitamin C (ascorbic acid) is a water-soluble vitamin. It helps form and maintain the material that holds living cells together and strengthens the walls of blood vessels. It also helps normal tooth and bone formation and builds resistance to bacterial infection.

Natural vitamin C and commercially produced ascorbic acid are chemically the same substance.

Natural sources of vitamin C (citrus fruits, tomatoes, white potatoes, sweet potatoes, and green leafy vegetables) add other nutrients besides C and provide bulk, necessary for good digestion.

How much vitamin C is needed each day? One-half grapefruit (or six ounces of orange juice) plus a serving of a vegetable high in C will meet the daily requirement. As the body does not store this vitamin, moderate amounts of C-rich foods must be eaten daily.

The B Vitamins

All of the B-complex vitamins are vital to normal metabolism and good health. All the B vitamins are water-soluble, like vitamin C, which means they are not stored in the body and must be taken daily. The Bs help metabolize carbohydrates and provide energy. Each of the B vitamins has additional special functions.

Thiamine—Thiamine plays an important part in carbohydrate metabolism and in the functioning of the nervous system. It also helps digestion and a normal appetite. Thiamine deficiency causes beriberi. Pork and liver are particularly good sources of thiamine.

Riboflavin—Riboflavin also promotes metabolism. A deficiency in riboflavin causes sore lips, tongue, and mouth, and rough scaly skin. The eyes are also affected by lack of riboflavin. Liver is an excellent source of this vitamin.

Niacin—Niacin helps the body metabolize the nutrients in food. A lack of niacin can cause pellegra, which can be fatal. The proper amounts of protein give us the niacin we need.

Pyridoxine—B_6 is a part of the enzyme system that helps us use and build protein. Meat, whole grain cereals, dried beans, potatoes, and dark green leafy vegetables are good B_6 providers.

Pantothenic Acid—Pantothenic acid also plays a part in the chemical processes that keep us moving and working. Foods that supply the other Bs are good sources of pantothenic acid.

Biotin—Biotin is available in organ or variety meats, muscle meats, milk, vegetables, egg yolks, grains, and some fruits. It works in several enzyme systems.

Folacin and B_{12}—Folacin and B_{12} are particularly important in formation of red blood cells. Green leafy vegetables, liver, legumes, meat, whole grains, and other vegetables give us folacin. Organ and muscle meats, milk, cheese, and eggs take care of our B_{12} needs.

Choline—Probably not a true B vitamin, choline is made in the body from an amino acid with the help of B_{12} and folacin. It is available in a variety of foods.

Vitamin A

Vitamin A, a fat-soluble vitamin, can be stored in the body. It helps normal bone growth, it helps the eyes adjust to dim light, and it helps provide infection-resistant skin. It need not be consumed every day, but it is wise to eat A-rich foods every other day.

Vitamin A is found in animal foods only, such as liver, eggs, butter, whole milk, and cheese. Carotene changes into vitamin A after digestion. Dark green and deep yellow vegetables and deep yellow fruits are good carotene sources.

Vitamin D

Vitamin D helps the body to use calcium and phosphorus—strong bones and teeth are the result. Rickets is the soft-bone disease caused by deficiences of vitamin D, calcium, and phosphorus. Some D is found in egg yolk, butter, and liver; but some fish, particularly sardines, salmon, herring, and tuna, are more abundant sources of vitamin D. Milk that has been fortified with D is the most common source of this vitamin.

Vitamin K

Another of the fat-soluble vitamins, K is best known for its work in the normal clotting of blood and functioning of the liver. Several foods—green leafy vegetables, egg yolk, and organ meats—supply vitamin K. Some vitamin K is produced by bacteria in the intestinal tract.

Vitamin E

Vitamin E is a fat-soluble vitamin whose most important feature is its antioxidant properties. It prevents the unwanted oxidation of polyunsaturated fatty acids. Vitamin E is stored in the body in muscles and in fat deposits. E is found in many common foods: unsaturated fats, wheat germ and wheat germ oil, leafy vegetables, legumes, whole grains, liver, butter, milk, and eggs.

MINERALS

Certain minerals are necessary for the proper functioning of the human body. They give strength and rigidity to certain body tissues and help with a number of body functions. The tiny amounts of minerals required by the body have definite limits. Excesses can be toxic. Minerals work with each other in many different combinations. Each has a specific purpose, but a mineral seldom acts all by itself.

Calcium

Ninety-nine percent of the calcium in the body is in the skeleton—98 percent in the bones, 1 percent in the teeth. It helps blood clot and helps nerves and muscles, including the heart, react normally. Our need for calcium is lifelong—20 percent is replaced each year. Children and pregnant or nursing women need more calcium than other people.

Milk and milk products are our greatest sources of calcium. Fish bones such as those eaten in sardines and dark green leafy vegetables are sources of calcium, too. Most of the daily requirement of calcium for an adult is provided by just two glasses of milk a day or its equivalent.

Iron

Iron combines with protein to make hemoglobin, which carries oxygen in the blood from the lungs to the muscles, brain, and elsewhere. Iron helps cells use oxygen. Lack of iron can cause iron-deficiency anemia which, in turn, can cause lack of sleep, energy, and appetite. Organ meats (liver, kidney, heart) and red meats are great iron sources. Oysters, eggs, whole grain and enriched cereals, dried fruits (especially raisins and prunes), dark green leafy vegetables, dried beans, peas, and nuts supply some iron, too.

Phosphorus

Ninety percent of the body's phosphorus is deposited as inorganic phosphate in the bones and teeth. The other 10 percent is located in cells as organic phosphorus. Phosphorus is found in many of the same foods that provide calcium and protein foods.

Iodine

The thyroid gland needs iodine to make thyroxin, the regulator of certain body processes. Iodine shortages can cause goiter (enlarged thyroid). Anyone who has lived in the American Midwest knows that it is called the "Goiter Belt" because of its great distance from the sea, the major source of iodine. The addition of iodine to salt has helped prevent goiter.

Fluorine

Fluorine is the name of the pure element. When in solution or combination with other materials, it is called fluoride. It helps prevent tooth decay, and it also helps develop stronger bones.

Fluoridation of community water supplies has been endorsed by the American Dental Association and leading medical groups. Dentists can also supply a fluoride compound directly to the teeth. If you aren't sure whether there is fluoride in your water supply, check with your dentist.

Sodium, Potassium, Chlorine

These three minerals help in the transport of fluids in and out of cells and in the maintenance of a normal balance of water between fluids and cells. Sodium and potassium are vital to normal nerve responses and muscle contractions (including the heart). Sodium, potassium, and chlorine are essen-

tial in maintaining the balance of acid and alkali of the blood.

Sulfur, Copper, Cobalt, Molybdenum, Manganese, Selenium, and Zinc

Sulfur is active in every cell of the body and is an integral part of sulfur-containing amino acids. Copper works hand in hand with iron to make hemoglobin in the blood. Iron needs copper to work with. All of these elements are in adequate supply in the normal diet. Supplementation, other than under a doctor's care, could be dangerous.

WATER

The human body is one half to two thirds water—ten gallons in an adult male. Water is absolutely necessary for life. It is the solvent for everything that we digest. It holds nutrients in solution, carries them through the blood stream, and is an important part of every cell structure. It carries away waste materials, controls the body's temperature, aids digestion, and sustains the health of all cells.

Water is provided largely by the fluids we drink, whether it is water itself or other liquids. Many foods contain a lot of water, too. Nutritionists recommend drinking two quarts of water a day.

FOUR FOOD GROUPS

Now that you understand a little of the what, why, and how of nutrients, how do you apply that information to daily eating patterns?

The "Basic Four" classification is now the basis of most nutrition education in the United States.

DAILY FOOD GUIDE

By Food Groups	child	pre-teen & teen	adult	aging adult
MILK GROUP cups of milk or equivalents	3–4	4 or more	2	2
MEAT GROUP 3 oz. serving meat, fish, shellfish or poultry; 2 eggs; 1 cup cooked dried beans, peas or lentils; ¼ cup peanut butter	1–2	3 or more	2	2
FRUIT AND VEGETABLE GROUP servings of C-rich fruits and vegetables	1	1–2	1	1–2
servings of A-rich fruits and vegetables	1	2	1	1
servings of potatoes, other fruits and vegetables	2	1	2	0–1
BREAD AND CEREAL GROUP servings of whole grain or enriched bread or cereal, baked goods, macaroni	3–4	4 or more	3–4	2–3
OTHER tablespoons of fat (oil, butter, margarine)	2	2–4	2–3	1–2

Water or liquid equivalent to make 3 to 5 cups total daily intake.

(Chart adapted from American Medical Association and reprinted with permission.)

In this classification, foods are divided into four categories according to their similarity in nutrient content. The groups are the Milk Group, the Meat Group, the Fruit and Vegetable Group, and the Bread and Cereal Group. Other foods that fall outside these four categories are included in an additional or Other Group.

MILK GROUP
The Milk Group includes all types of milk and milk products except butter and cream. These milk products are ice cream, cheese, and yogurt.

Milk is our main source of calcium. It also supplies phosphorus, protein, riboflavin, and vitamins A and D. Lowfat milks are fortified with vitamin A, and all milk you buy should be fortified with vitamin D. Foods from the milk group help promote the development of strong bones and teeth, healthy skin and tissue, good night vision, and a well-running nervous system.

Cheese, ice cream, and milk used in cream soups, sauces, puddings, or in other cooking all count towards the daily number of servings of milk. Cream and butter should be considered part of the Other Group.

MEAT GROUP
The Meat Group includes beef, lamb, veal, pork,

variety meats (liver, kidney, brains, and heart), poultry, eggs, fish, and shellfish. Meat alternates or substitutes are dried beans and peas (soy, pinto, navy, lima, kidney beans, chickpeas, split or black-eye peas), lentils, nuts, and peanut butter.

Foods from the Meat Group supply protein, iron, and the B vitamins (especially thiamine, niacin, and riboflavin). Two or more servings of meat a day are recommended. Preferably, something from the meat group should be included at each meal.

FRUIT AND VEGETABLE GROUP

All fruits and vegetables fall in this group, but special emphasis goes to those that are good sources of vitamins C and A. Fruits and vegetables also supply other vitamins, minerals, and carbohydrates—all at little calorie cost. In addition, they add bulk.

Meals and snacks should include four or more servings from this group every day. One of those four must be a good source of vitamin C (or two servings of foods containing lesser amounts of C). One serving every other day should be a good source of vitamin A. A serving is usually one-half cup of the fruit or vegetable or an equivalent amount.

BREAD AND CEREAL GROUP

Enriched, whole grain, or restored breads, cooked or dry cereals, cornmeal, crackers, flour, grits, macaroni, spaghetti, noodles, rice, rolled oats, baked goods, bulgur, or parboiled rice or wheat are all members of the Bread and Cereal Group.

Breads and cereals are an excellent source of carbohydrates, iron, and those important B vitamins. Three to four servings should be eaten daily. Check the labels—products that are not enriched, not whole grain, nor restored don't count! If one of the servings is not a cereal, have an extra serving of enriched or whole grain bread or baked goods. A serving is one slice bread, one ounce (about a cup) ready-to-eat cereal, or its equivalent in other cereals.

OTHER GROUP

Many of the foods in the Other Group are fun foods. Examples are sugars (candy, soft drinks, gelatin desserts, alcoholic beverages, and syrup), salad dressings, cream, butter, margarine, oils, and other fats.

These foods contribute fat, sugar, seasoning, and calories to our diets. They add flavor to other foods and help us meet our energy needs. Except for the recommended amounts of fat, they are not essential to a healthy diet.

SPECIAL NEEDS FOR SPECIAL PEOPLE

Everybody needs the same nutrients, but some people need more than others because of special demands on their bodies at various times in their lives.

Prenatal care obviously depends on the kind of nutrition the mother gets. Nursing infants and preschool children also have special nutritional needs. For young school children, a good breakfast has been shown to be essential to success in school. The poor eating habits of teen-agers, especially girls, are legendary and must be avoided. Senior citizens need fewer calories, but not less nutrition. Careful food selection can help prolong a healthy, happy life—even on a restricted budget. Special diets, such as for diabetes, are by definition "special." There is only one safe way to approach them: consult your physician and follow his advice.

U.S. RDA AND NUTRITION LABELING

U.S. RDA stands for "United States Recommended Daily Allowances." The U.S. RDAs were developed by the Food and Drug Administration (FDA) for its nutrition labeling and dietary supplement programs, and were derived from the Recommended Daily Dietary Allowances of the Food and Nutrition Board of the National Academy of Sciences. The U.S. RDAs represent amounts of protein, vitamins, and minerals that will fully satisfy a healthy adult's daily needs for these nutrients. Many adults may need only three fourths of the U.S. RDA for several nutrients, and children

RECOMMENDED DAILY DIETARY ALLOWANCES (Abridged),* Revised 1973

| | Years | | Weight | | Height | | Energy | Protein | Vitamins | | | | | Minerals | |
	From	Up to	(kg)	(lbs)	(cm)	(in)	(calories)	(g)	Vitamin A (IU)	Ascorbic Acid (mg)	Niacin (mg)	Riboflavin (mg)	Thiamine (mg)	Calcium (mg)	Iron (mg)
Infants	0.0–0.5		6	14	60	24	kg × 117	kg × 2.2	1,400	35	5	0.4	0.3	360	10
	0.5–1.0		9	20	71	28	kg × 108	kg × 2.0	2,000	35	8	0.6	0.5	540	15
Children	1–3		13	28	86	34	1300	23	2,000	40	9	0.8	0.7	800	15
	4–6		20	44	110	44	1800	30	2,500	40	12	1.1	0.9	800	10
	7–10		30	66	135	54	2400	36	3,300	40	16	1.2	1.2	800	10
Males	11–14		44	97	158	63	2800	44	5,000	45	18	1.5	1.4	1200	18
	15–18		61	134	172	69	3000	54	5,000	45	20	1.8	1.5	1200	18
	19–22		67	147	172	69	3000	52	5,000	45	20	1.8	1.5	800	10
	23–50		70	154	172	69	2700	56	5,000	45	18	1.6	1.4	800	10
	51+		70	154	172	69	2400	56	5,000	45	16	1.5	1.2	800	10
Females	11–14		44	97	155	62	2400	44	4,000	45	16	1.3	1.2	1200	18
	15–18		54	119	162	65	2100	48	4,000	45	14	1.4	1.1	1200	18
	19–22		58	128	162	65	2100	46	4,000	45	14	1.4	1.1	800	18
	23–50		58	128	162	65	2000	46	4,000	45	13	1.2	1.0	800	18
	51+		58	128	162	65	1800	46	4,000	45	12	1.1	1.0	800	10
Pregnant							+300	+30	5,000	60	+2	+0.3	+0.3	1200	18+
Lactating							+500	+20	6,000	60	+4	+0.5	+0.3	1200	18

* The allowances are amounts of nutrients recommended by the Food and Nutrition Board, National Academy of Sciences—National Research Council. They are intended to provide for individual variations among most normal persons as they live in the United States under usual environmental stresses. Diets should be based on a variety of common foods in order to provide other nutrients for which human requirements have been less well defined. The Recommended Daily Dietary Allowances, which in unabridged form cover 16 vitamins and minerals, are revised from time to time in accordance with newer knowledge of nutritional needs.

may need only about one half. Thus the U.S. RDAs are only a guideline for good nutrition and are intended primarily for use in nutrition labeling.

The information given on nutrition labels will help you plan more nutritious meals, help you compare nutritive values of different brands, and help you in selecting foods for special diets.

FOOD ADDITIVES

A food additive is any substance added to foods during processing or packaging. Most additives are in chemical form, derived from natural substances. Food additives are nothing new. Salt and pepper have been used for centuries for the preservation of meat. Spices and herbs are also additives.

In order to be used as a food additive, a substance must be safe in the quantity used, it must perform its intended function, and it must not jeopardize the nutritional value of the food.

Without additives our foods would cost more and probably be less wholesome. Furthermore, the laws in the United States governing food quality and the use of food additives are the strictest in the world. Nevertheless, since some food additives remain insufficiently tested, many questions regarding their safety have yet to be answered.

WEIGHT CONTROL

Library shelves and bookstores are filled with books about weight control, because many people are concerned with overweight. This concern is justified. Obesity, the condition in which too much of the body is composed of fat, is a serious health problem.

If you are overweight and serious about losing extra pounds, the solution is simple—consume fewer calories and get more exercise. Do this on a moderate, regular schedule—no crash or fad diets and no furious exercise programs. It takes 3,500 calories to make one pound of body fat, so by cutting only 500 calories a day, a dieter can lose one pound in a week. This is a safe amount to lose and an effective way to diet.

Cutting down on calories does not mean cutting down on nutrition. A wise weight-control diet will be based on the Four Food Groups. Accumulating extra weight is a long-term process, and so is getting rid of it. Just as gaining extra pounds is due largely to poor eating habits, losing them will depend upon developing new eating habits—habits that once established ought to last a lifetime.

MEAL PLANNING

Planning for nutritionally balanced, appetizing meals will become second nature to you if you understand the Four Food Groups and use the guidelines of the Daily Food Guide. Put together a variety of foods from the four groups, adding from the Other Group for flavor and fun, and you can hardly go wrong. Try to include foods that have well-rounded nutrient personalities, with a combination of food values (protein, calories, vitamins, minerals, etc.). Choose foods wisely so you benefit from everything you eat.

Breakfast should provide at least one fourth of the daily food needs. If the usual breakfast foods leave you cold, try an appealing array of cheeses, muffins or breads, fruits, and yogurt. After all, lox, cream cheese, and bagels are a common breakfast combination.

Make lunch worth something by selecting a meat, fish, or egg sandwich (on enriched or whole grain bread). Add something from the Fruit and Vegetable Group as a garnish or go-with. Cheese, fruit, and enriched bread or crackers are even easier to fix and still supply what you need to get on with the day.

Usually the evening meal is planned around a main dish. A green or yellow vegetable, rich in vitamins, will complement any main dish. Salads and breads are frequent accompaniments to dinners and suppers. Vary the greens you use in tossed salads. When a tossed salad doesn't seem to fit the bill, offer fruit salad, cole slaw, or a relish tray. Muffins, biscuits, or French bread can add a special touch to a meal, too. Desserts should be chosen to complement the dinner. Choose a light dessert, such as sherbet or fruit, to follow a heavy meal.

CALORIES FOR ACTIVITIES

Type of Activity	Calories per hour
Sedentary activities, such as: Reading; writing; eating; watching television or movies; listening to the radio; sewing; playing cards; and typing, miscellaneous officework, and other activities done while sitting that require little or no arm movement	80 to 100
Light activities, such as: Preparing and cooking food; doing dishes; dusting; handwashing small articles of clothing; ironing; walking slowly; personal care; miscellaneous officework and other activities done while standing that require some arm movement; and rapid typing and other activities done while sitting that are more strenuous.	110 to 160
Moderate activities, such as: Making beds; mopping and scrubbing; sweeping; light polishing and waxing; laundering by machine; light gardening and carpentry work; walking moderately fast; other activities done while standing that require moderate arm movement; and activities done while sitting that require more vigorous arm movement.	170 to 240
Vigorous activities, such as: Heavy scrubbing and waxing; handwashing large articles of clothing; hanging out clothes; stripping beds; other heavy work; walking fast; bowling; golfing; and gardening.	250 to 350
Strenuous activities, such as: Swimming; playing tennis; running; bicycling; dancing; skiing; and playing football.	350 and more

SHOPPING

Concentrate on your shopping. For the time that you are in the store it is your profession. Bring along the list of foods you plan to buy for use during the week. Remember the purpose of the list and stick to it. Ignore those sudden impulses; remember the time you spent planning, and go by that plan. It is a good idea to eat before you go to the market. If you shop hungry, you may be tempted to buy more than you need, especially snack-type foods.

Read labels, check unit pricing, and buy grades to match your purposes. Private or "house" brands are usually less expensive than name brands. Remember also, that you are shopping for food, not for beauty.

A USDA publication, *Your Money's Worth in Foods,* is a helpful reference for budgeting, menu planning, and shopping. It includes charts and tables of costs per serving and per pound, and cost-weight tables to compare costs of foods from different-sized containers. Knowing the cost per serving is especially important when meat shopping.

After shopping, go directly home. Do nonfood errands before you get to the supermarket. Perishables lose food value quickly if they are not promptly and properly cared for.

STORING

Unpack, sort, and store foods carefully. Nonperishables in unopened packages are best kept in cool, dark places. After opening, certain items must be refrigerated—the label will tell. Carefully wrap and clearly label all foods that you will not

Piquant Cheese Loaf, 26;
Date Nut Bread, 27;
Bran Rolls, 25

use until later. Storing food is more than just setting it aside for later use. Storing improperly can waste nutritive values.

Nutrition is lost when foods spoil, and poor planning is the cause of waste. Try to cook just the right amounts of food, and if you do have leftovers, use them right away.

FOOD SAFETY

How you handle food is important. Careful handling of food can help prevent sickness and can even be a matter of life or death. Most food poisoning is the result of inadequate sanitary precautions in the kitchen.

A clean, dry kitchen and a clean cook are the best precautions you can take, Tuck away your hair and wear clean clothes. Hands should be clean and dry. Wash them after touching nonfood items, after handling each particular food, and especially after handling each raw food. If you have a cut or infection on your hands, wear rubber or plastic gloves. No coughing or sneezing near food, please. If you are sick you shouldn't be cooking.

Bacteria like warm, moist, cozy spots to grow and reproduce in. Bacteria are likely to be found wherever food is or has been. Sometimes bacteria just spoil food, but sometimes they create toxins that can spoil us. To control bacteria and their growth, wash foods before preparing them. This includes poultry, meat, fruits, vegetables, and eggs in the shell.

COOKING TO CONSERVE NUTRITIVE VALUES

Sensible storage can save nutrients; careful preparation and cooking can, too. Happily, cooking to save nutrients not only gives you the best of the food, but is the easiest of all methods—simple and short. By cooking quickly, with a minimum of preparation, you save time, steps, and nutrients. As a bonus, you get food that looks, tastes, feels, and *is* better. A special note: extra precautions are needed to prevent loss of vitamins. Heat only to serving temperatures and use a minimum amount of water.

It's our hope that, using the Nutrition Know-How information provided on these pages and the recipes that follow, you'll find planning and preparing nutritious meals easy and rewarding.

Soups

Serve a steaming mug of soup on a cold day, or serve it chilled on a hot summer evening. Soup can be an elegant introduction to the entrée or a wonderful main dish. Anyone from beginner to experienced cook can create delicious soups easily and from simple ingredients.

Soups make use of a wide variety of nutritional foods and can be excellent sources of vitamins, proteins, and minerals. The stocks for most soups are easy to make. In many of the following recipes they are created during cooking. In those recipes calling for broth or bouillon, you may use home-made stock, canned broth, or bouillon cubes. Herbs, spices, and other flavorings will enhance the taste of any soup, and garnishes provide an attractive final touch.

Baked Ripe Olive Minestrone

1½ pounds lean beef for stew, cut in
     1¼-inch cubes
  1 cup coarsely chopped onion
  1 teaspoon minced garlic
  1 teaspoon salt
 ¼ teaspoon ground black pepper
  2 tablespoons olive oil
  3 cans (10½ ounces each) condensed
     beef broth
  2 soup cans water
1½ teaspoons herb seasoning
  1 can (16 ounces) tomatoes
     (undrained)
  1 can (15¼ ounces) kidney beans
     (undrained)
  1 can (6 ounces) pitted ripe olives
     (undrained)
1½ cups thinly sliced carrots
  1 cup small seashell macaroni
  2 cups sliced zucchini
     Grated Parmesan cheese

1. Mix beef, onion, garlic, salt, and pepper in a Dutch oven or saucepot. Add olive oil and stir to coat meat evenly.
2. Set in a 400°F oven about 40 minutes, stirring once or twice.
3. Reduce heat to 350°F. Add broth, water, and herb seasoning; stir. Cover; cook 1 hour, or until meat is almost tender.
4. Remove from oven and stir in tomatoes and kidney beans with liquid, ripe olives with liquid, carrots, and macaroni. Put sliced zucchini on top. Cover Dutch oven and return to oven 30 to 40 minutes, or until carrots are tender.
5. Ladle hot soup into bowls. Serve with grated cheese.

About 3½ quarts soup

Potato Soup

6 medium (about 2 pounds) potatoes,
  pared and cut in ¼-inch slices
5 cups cold water
1 carrot, pared and cut in pieces
1 leek, washed thoroughly and thinly
  sliced (white part only)
1 stalk celery, cut in pieces
1 medium onion, cut in slices
2 teaspoons salt
¼ teaspoon ground white pepper
¼ teaspoon ground thyme
¼ teaspoon ground marjoram
1 bay leaf
1 beef bouillon cube
2 tablespoons butter or margarine
3 tablespoons flour
  Fresh parsley, snipped

1. Put potatoes and water into a large heavy saucepan. Cover and bring to boiling. Reduce heat to medium and add carrot, leek, celery, onion, salt, pepper, thyme, marjoram, and bay leaf. Cover; bring to boiling, reduce heat, and simmer about 1 hour, or until vegetables are tender.
2. With a slotted spoon, remove the carrot, leek, celery, onion, and bay leaf; discard. Remove 1 cup of the potato broth and add beef bouillon cube; stir until dissolved.
3. Force remaining potato mixture through a fine sieve into saucepan.
4. Heat butter in a saucepan. Blend in flour. Heat until bubbly. Add the 1 cup of potato broth gradually, stirring constantly. Pour into the soup and blend well. Bring to boiling, reduce heat, and simmer 5 to 10 minutes.
5. Ladle hot soup into bowls. Garnish with parsley.

About 2½ pints soup

Fresh Vegetable Beef Soup

Beef broth (about 4½ quarts):
3 tablespoons butter or margarine
3 . pounds beef shank cross cuts
1 clove garlic, peeled
2 onions, peeled and cut in quarters
4 pieces celery with leaves
4 tomatoes, cut in wedges
2 carrots, pared and cut in pieces
1 bay leaf
1½ teaspoons thyme leaves
2 parsley sprigs
4 beef bouillon cubes
6 peppercorns
1 tablespoon salt
4½ quarts water

Vegetables for soup:
1½ cups sliced celery
1½ cups sliced pared carrots
3 cups chopped cabbage
2 cups fresh green beans, cut in
  1-inch pieces
4 tomatoes, peeled and chopped
4 large potatoes, pared and cut in
  1-inch cubes
1½ cups fresh corn kernels
1 tablespoon salt

1. For broth, heat butter in a large kettle. Add beef shank and brown on all sides. Add garlic, onions, celery, tomatoes, carrots, herbs, bouillon cubes, peppercorns, salt, and water. Cover; bring to boiling, reduce heat, and simmer about 2 hours.
2. Remove meat. Strain broth and return broth to kettle. Cut meat into small pieces and add to broth.
3. For soup, add celery, carrots, cabbage, green beans, tomatoes, potatoes, corn, and salt to broth. Cover; bring to boiling, reduce heat, and simmer 30 minutes, or until vegetables are tender.
4. Ladle hot soup into bowls.

About 5½ quarts soup

Easy Vegetable Soup

1 can (15½ ounces) green beans
(undrained)
1 package (10 ounces) frozen
chopped broccoli, defrosted and
separated
4 cups shredded cabbage
2 cups chopped celery
4½ cups beef broth (homemade,
canned, or from bouillon cubes)
2 tablespoons instant minced onion
2 cups tomato juice

1. Put green beans with liquid, broccoli, cabbage, celery, beef broth, and onion into a large saucepan or Dutch oven.
2. Cover; bring to boiling, reduce heat, and simmer 15 minutes, or until vegetables are tender. Stir in tomato juice. Heat thoroughly.
3. Ladle hot soup into bowls.

About 2½ quarts soup

Cream of Fresh Mushroom Soup

¼ cup butter or margarine
2 tablespoons chopped onion
½ cup enriched flour
½ teaspoon salt
⅛ teaspoon ground pepper
Few grains cayenne pepper
3 cups chicken broth (homemade,
canned, or from bouillon cubes)
8 ounces fresh mushrooms, cleaned
and sliced lengthwise
2 cups milk, scalded
2 tablespoons sherry
Fresh parsley, snipped

1. Heat butter in a saucepan. Mix in onion and cook until crisp-tender. Mix in flour, salt, and peppers. Add chicken broth gradually, stirring constantly. Continue to stir, bring to boiling, and cook 1 minute. Stir in mushrooms. Cover; cook over low heat 30 minutes, stirring occasionally.
2. Remove cover and stir in scalded milk. Cook, uncovered, over low heat 5 to 10 minutes.
3. Just before serving, mix in the sherry. Garnish with parsley.

About 2½ pints soup

Oyster Soup

6 tablespoons butter or margarine
2 tablespoons flour
2 teaspoons salt
2 cups milk
4 small carrots, pared and finely
diced
2 small turnips, pared and finely
diced
4 celery stalks, finely diced
1 pint oysters (undrained)
¼ teaspoon ground black pepper
2 cups cream, heated just until hot
1 teaspoon Worcestershire sauce
Fresh parsley, snipped

1. Heat 2 tablespoons butter in a saucepan. Blend in flour and ½ teaspoon salt. Heat until bubbly. Add milk gradually, stirring constantly. Bring to boiling; cook 1 to 2 minutes. Set aside and keep warm.
2. Heat 2 tablespoons butter in a skillet. Add carrots, turnips, and celery and cook until just tender, stirring frequently. Remove from heat and set aside.
3. Heat 2 tablespoons butter in a saucepan. Add oysters with liquor, 1½ teaspoons salt, and pepper. Simmer 3 minutes, or until oysters are plump and edges begin to curl.
4. Blend cream with the white sauce. Stir in Worcestershire sauce, vegetables, and oyster mixture.
5. Ladle hot soup into bowls. Sprinkle with parsley.

About 2 quarts soup

Lentil Soup

¼ cup olive oil
1 cup chopped onion
1 cup diced green pepper
¼ cup diced pimento
2 tablespoons flour
1 pound dried lentils, rinsed
1 can (16 ounces) tomatoes
   (undrained)
2 cups diagonally sliced carrots
1 cup diagonally sliced celery
1 tablespoon salt
8 cups water

1. Heat olive oil in a Dutch oven or saucepot. Add onion, green pepper, and pimento; cook, stirring occasionally, until soft. Blend in flour and heat until bubbly. Add lentils, tomatoes with liquid, carrots, celery, salt, and water; stir.
2. Cover; bring to boiling, reduce heat, and simmer 2 hours, stirring as necessary.
3. Ladle hot soup into bowls.

About 3 quarts soup

Lima Soy Bean Soup

1 pound dried baby lima beans,
   rinsed
6 cups water
1 cup dried soy beans, rinsed
¾ cup water
3 medium onions, peeled and
   chopped
1 pound smoked shoulder roll (butt)
   or smoked ham (with skin and
   fat trimmed and reserved), cut
   in small cubes
4 cups water
1 teaspoon salt
¼ teaspoon pepper
2 tablespoons prepared mustard

1. Put lima beans into a large saucepot or Dutch oven. Add 6 cups water. Bring to boiling and boil rapidly 2 minutes. Cover tightly, remove from heat, and set aside about 1 hour.
2. Put soy beans into a saucepan and add enough water to cover. Cover saucepan; bring to boiling, reduce heat, and cook 30 minutes.
3. Drain and rinse soy beans. Return beans to saucepan and add water to cover. Bring to boiling and cook 30 minutes. Drain and rinse beans.
4. Put soy beans into an electric blender container with ¾ cup water. Cover; blend until puréed. Set aside.
5. Put onions, meat cubes, skin, fat, and 4 cups water into saucepot with lima beans. Cover; bring to boiling and simmer 1 hour, stirring as necessary.
6. Mix in the soy bean purée, salt, pepper, and prepared mustard. Cook 30 minutes, or until lima beans are tender. Remove and discard meat skin and fat.
7. Ladle hot soup into bowls.

About 4 quarts soup

Blender Pea Soup

1 can (17 ounces) green peas
   (undrained)
1½ cups milk
2 tablespoons butter or margarine
2 teaspoons flour
½ teaspoon salt
½ teaspoon monosodium glutamate
½ teaspoon ground nutmeg
¼ teaspoon sugar
1 small onion, quartered
   Lemon pepper
   marinade (optional)

1. Put green peas with liquid, 1 cup milk, butter, flour, salt, monosodium glutamate, nutmeg, and sugar into an electric blender container. Cover and blend thoroughly. Remove cover and add onion, a quarter at a time, continuing to blend.
2. Pour mixture into a heavy saucepan.
3. Use the remaining ½ cup milk to rinse out blender (cover blender and turn on, then off). Pour into the saucepan. Bring to boiling, stirring occasionally.
4. Ladle hot soup into mugs. Sprinkle, if desired, with lemon pepper marinade.

About 1 quart soup

Breads

Breads are generally divided into two groups: quick breads and yeast breads. The quick breads include muffins, biscuits, and many kinds of nut and fruit breads. They are quick to mix up—indeed, the one rule for quick breads is not to overmix. The second group of breads uses the slower-working yeast as a riser.

Homemade breads are valuable sources of vitamins and minerals. Many of the following recipes call for enriched all-purpose flour, available in all supermarkets. Whole wheat flour and bran are used in many of these recipes. Cornmeal, rye, oats, and wheat germ are other healthful grain products in some of these breads. Keep flours and grain products on hand and you'll always be ready to make up that fresh loaf of bread.

Refrigerator Bran Muffins

3 cups whole bran cereal
1 cup boiling water
½ cup shortening
1½ cups sugar
2 eggs
2 cups buttermilk
3 cups sifted enriched all-purpose flour
2½ teaspoons baking soda
½ teaspoon salt

1. Put bran cereal into a bowl. Pour in boiling water. Set aside until cool.
2. Put shortening and sugar into a large mixer bowl. Beat until thoroughly blended. Beat in eggs one at a time. Alternately mix in the soaked bran and buttermilk.
3. Sift flour, baking soda, and salt together; add to the bran mixture and mix gently until ingredients are thoroughly moistened (do not overmix).
4. Pour batter into well-greased 2½ × 1¼-inch muffin-pan wells, filling each about two-thirds full.
5. Bake at 400°F 15 to 18 minutes. Immediately loosen and tip muffins in wells. Serve warm.
6. Batter may be stored in tightly covered jars in a refrigerator as long as 3 weeks; when ready to bake, pour batter into muffin-pan wells and proceed as above.

About 3 dozen muffins

Baking Powder Biscuits

2 cups sifted enriched all-purpose
    flour
1 tablespoon baking powder
1 teaspoon salt
⅓ cup lard or other shortening
¾ cup milk
    Milk for brushing tops

1. Sift flour, baking powder, and salt together into a bowl. Add lard and cut in with a pastry blender or two knives until mixture resembles coarse cornmeal. Add milk and stir with a fork until a dough is formed.
2. Turn dough onto a lightly floured surface. Shape into a ball and knead lightly 10 to 15 times. Gently roll dough ½ inch thick. Cut with a floured biscuit cutter or knife, using an even pressure to keep sides of biscuits straight.
3. Place on ungreased cookie sheet, close together for soft-sided biscuits or 1 inch apart for crusty sides. Brush tops lightly with milk.
4. Bake at 450°F 10 to 15 minutes.

About 1 dozen biscuits

Buttermilk Biscuits: Follow recipe for Baking Powder Biscuits; decrease baking powder to 2½ teaspoons and add ¼ **teaspoon baking soda** to dry ingredients. Substitute **buttermilk** for milk.

Cornbread

1 cup sifted enriched all-purpose
    flour
¼ cup sugar
1 tablespoon baking powder
¾ teaspoon salt
1 cup enriched yellow cornmeal
¼ cup melted shortening, butter, or
    margarine
1 egg, well beaten
1 cup milk

1. Sift flour, sugar, baking powder, and salt together into a bowl; mix in cornmeal.
2. Combine melted shortening, egg, and milk. Add liquid mixture to flour mixture; beat just until smooth. Turn batter into a greased 8×8×2-inch pan and spread to corners.
3. Bake at 425°F about 20 minutes. Cut into squares and serve warm.

9 servings

Crisp Corn Sticks: Follow recipe for Cornbread. Spoon batter into 12 greased hot cornstick pan sections, filling each three-fourths full. Bake 10 to 15 minutes.

Lemony Apple Nut Bread

¼ cup butter or margarine
⅔ cup sugar
2 eggs, well beaten
2 cups sifted enriched all-purpose
    flour
1 teaspoon baking powder
1 teaspoon baking soda
1 teaspoon salt
2 cups coarsely grated pared cooking
    apples
⅔ cup chopped walnuts
1 tablespoon grated lemon peel

1. Cream butter in a bowl; add sugar gradually, mixing until light and fluffy. Beat in eggs.
2. Sift flour, baking powder, baking soda, and salt together. Add flour mixture alternately with apples to creamed mixture, mixing until blended after each addition. Stir in walnuts and grated lemon peel. Turn into a greased 9×5×3-inch loaf pan and spread evenly.
3. Bake at 350°F 45 to 50 minutes.
4. Cool bread 10 minutes in pan on wire rack; remove from pan and cool completely before slicing or storing.

1 loaf bread

Whole Wheat Pear Bread

2 to 3 fresh Bartlett pears
2 tablespoons shortening
1 teaspoon grated lemon peel
⅔ cup firmly packed light brown
 sugar
½ cup honey
2 tablespoons lemon juice
⅓ cup water
1 egg, beaten
1 cup sifted enriched all-purpose
 flour
1 teaspoon baking soda
1 teaspoon salt
½ teaspoon ground cinnamon
¼ teaspoon ground cloves
1 cup whole wheat flour
1 cup chopped walnuts

1. Core pears, but do not peel. Cut lengthwise slices from one pear and reserve to decorate top. Dice enough remaining pears to measure 1 cup.
2. Mix shortening, grated lemon peel, and brown sugar in a bowl. Add honey, lemon juice, water, and egg; mix well.
3. Sift all-purpose flour, baking soda, salt, cinnamon, and cloves; stir in whole wheat flour. Add flour mixture to liquid mixture; stir just enough to moisten flour. Mix in walnuts and diced pears. Turn into a greased 9×5×3-inch loaf pan and arrange reserved pear slices crosswise along center.
4. Bake at 325°F 70 to 75 minutes.
5. Cool bread 10 minutes in pan on wire rack; remove from pan and cool completely before slicing or storing.

1 loaf bread

Bran Rolls

¾ cup whole bran cereal
⅓ cup sugar
1½ teaspoons salt
½ cup margarine
½ cup boiling water
½ cup warm water
2 packages active dry yeast
1 egg, beaten
3¼ to 3¾ cups sifted enriched
 all-purpose flour
 Margarine, melted

1. Combine bran cereal, sugar, salt, and margarine in a bowl. Add boiling water; stir until margarine is melted. Cool to lukewarm.
2. Measure warm water into a warm large bowl. Sprinkle in yeast; stir until dissolved. Mix in lukewarm cereal mixture, egg, and enough of the flour to make a stiff dough.
3. Turn dough onto a lightly floured surface; knead 8 to 10 minutes, or until smooth and elastic. Form dough into a ball and place in a greased deep bowl; turn to bring greased surface to top. Cover; let rise in a warm place until double in bulk (about 1 hour).
4. Punch dough down; divide in half. Divide each half into 12 equal pieces. Form each piece into a smooth ball. Place in greased muffin-pan wells, 2½×1½ inches, or in 2 greased 8-inch round cake pans. Brush rolls with melted margarine. Cover; let rise again until double in bulk (about 30 minutes).
5. Bake at 375°F 20 to 25 minutes. Remove from pans and place on wire racks. Serve warm.

2 dozen rolls

Piquant Cheese Loaf

7 to 7¼ cups sifted enriched
    all-purpose flour
1 teaspoon sugar
1 tablespoon salt
2 packages active dry yeast
1 cup plain yogurt
½ cup water
2 tablespoons margarine
6 eggs (at room temperature)
½ pound muenster cheese, shredded
    (about 2 cups)
2 cups julienne cooked ham
    (optional)
1 egg, slightly beaten
1 tablespoon milk

1. Mix 1½ cups flour, sugar, salt, and undissolved yeast thoroughly in a large mixer bowl.
2. Combine yogurt, water, and margarine in a saucepan. Set over low heat until very warm (120–130°F); margarine does not need to melt. Add liquid mixture gradually to dry ingredients while beating at low speed of electric mixer. Beat at medium speed 2 minutes, scraping bowl occasionally. Add 6 eggs, 1 cup flour, and 1½ cups shredded cheese. Beat at high speed 2 minutes, scraping bowl occasionally. Stir in enough of the remaining flour to make a stiff dough.
3. Turn dough onto a lightly floured surface. Knead 8 to 10 minutes, or until dough is smooth, elastic, and shows small blisters under surface when drawn tight.
4. Form dough into a ball and place in greased deep bowl; turn to bring greased surface to top. Cover; let rise in a warm place until double in bulk (about 1 hour).
5. Punch down dough; turn onto lightly floured surface. Divide in half. If using ham, knead 1 cup ham strips into each half. Shape each half into a ball and place on a greased cookie sheet. Cover; let rise again until double in bulk (about 1 hour).
6. Combine egg and milk; brush over loaves. Sprinkle with remaining ½ cup cheese.
7. Bake at 350°F about 30 minutes. Remove from cookie sheets and place on wire racks to cool.

2 loaves bread

Whole Wheat Bread

2 packages active dry yeast
1 cup warm water
½ cup butter or margarine
⅓ cup dark molasses
4 teaspoons salt
1½ cups milk, scalded
4 cups whole wheat flour
3½ cups sifted enriched all-purpose
    flour

1. Soften yeast in warm water. Set aside.
2. Combine butter, molasses, salt, and milk in a large bowl; mix well. Cool to lukewarm.
3. Mix 1 cup whole wheat flour, then yeast, into liquid mixture. Add remaining whole wheat flour, 1 cup at a time, mixing after each addition. Add all-purpose flour gradually, beating until a stiff dough is formed.
4. Turn dough onto a lightly floured surface. Knead 10 minutes, or until dough is smooth and elastic. Cover; let rest 20 minutes.
5. Punch dough down and divide in half. Shape into loaves and place in greased 9×5×3-inch loaf pans. Cover; let rise in a warm place until double in bulk (1 hour).
6. Bake at 375°F 40 to 45 minutes. Remove from pans and place on wire racks to cool.

2 loaves bread

Raised Cornmeal Muffins

5 to 5¼ cups sifted enriched
    all-purpose flour
½ cup sugar
1 tablespoon salt
2 packages active dry yeast
2¼ cups milk
½ cup shortening
2 eggs
1 cup enriched yellow cornmeal
    Butter or margarine, melted

1. Mix 2¾ cups flour, sugar, salt, and undissolved yeast thoroughly in a large mixer bowl.
2. Put milk and shortening into a saucepan. Set over low heat until very warm (120–130°F). Add liquid mixture gradually to dry ingredients while mixing until blended. Beat 2 minutes at medium speed of electric mixer, scraping bowl occasionally. Mix in eggs and 1¾ cups flour, or enough to make a batter. Beat at high speed 2 minutes, scraping bowl occasionally. Blend in cornmeal and enough of the remaining flour to make a smooth, thick batter.
3. Cover; let rise in a warm place until double in bulk (1 to 1½ hours).
4. Beat batter down. Cut against side of bowl with a large spoon enough batter at one time to fill each greased 2½- or 3-inch muffin-pan well two-thirds full, pushing batter with a rubber spatula directly into well. Cover; let rise again until almost double in bulk (about 30 minutes).
5. Bake at 400°F about 20 minutes. Brush tops with melted butter. Remove from pans and serve piping hot.

1½ to 2 dozen muffins

Note: If desired, mix 1 teaspoon crushed herb, such as chervil, oregano, rosemary, or thyme with flour before adding to batter.

Date Nut Bread

½ cup warm water
2 packages active dry yeast
1¾ cups warm milk
2 tablespoons sugar
1 tablespoon salt
3 tablespoons margarine
5 to 5½ cups sifted enriched
    all-purpose flour
1 cup whole wheat flour
1 cup chopped dates
½ cup chopped pecans
1 teaspoon ground cinnamon
    Peanut oil
    Margarine (optional)

1. Measure warm water into a warm large bowl. Sprinkle in yeast; stir until dissolved. Add warm milk, sugar, salt, and margarine. Stir in 2 cups all-purpose flour. Beat with rotary beater until smooth (about 1 minute). Add 1 cup all-purpose flour; beat with rotary beater until smooth (about 1 minute). Add 1 cup all-purpose flour; beat vigorously with a wooden spoon until smooth (about 150 strokes). Stir in whole wheat flour, dates, pecans, cinnamon, and enough of the remaining all-purpose flour to make a soft dough.
2. Turn dough onto a lightly floured surface. Knead 8 to 10 minutes, or until dough is smooth, elastic, and shows small blisters under surface when drawn tight. Cover with plastic wrap, then a towel. Let rest 20 minutes.
3. Punch dough down. Divide into 3 equal portions. Roll each into a 12×7-inch rectangle. Shape into loaves. Place in 3 greased 7×4×2-inch loaf pans. Brush loaves with oil. Cover pans loosely with plastic wrap. Refrigerate 2 to 24 hours.
4. When ready to bake, remove loaves from refrigerator. Uncover dough carefully. Let stand uncovered 10 minutes at room temperature. Puncture with a greased wooden pick or metal skewer any gas bubbles which may have formed.
5. Bake at 400°F about 35 minutes. Remove from pans immediately, place on wire racks to cool, and, if desired, brush with margarine.

3 loaves bread

Prune-Wheat Coffee Cake

Filling:
- 1 cup snipped dried prunes
- ¾ cup water
- ¼ teaspoon ground allspice
- ¼ teaspoon ground cinnamon
- ½ teaspoon lemon juice
- ¼ cup honey
- ⅓ cup firmly packed brown sugar
- ½ cup sliced almonds

Dough:
- 1 package active dry yeast
- ½ cup warm water
- 2 tablespoons oil or melted shortening
- ⅓ cup honey
- 1¼ teaspoons salt
- ¾ cup milk
- 3½ to 4 cups whole wheat flour
- ½ cup finely chopped almonds

Topping:
- Confectioners' sugar (optional)

1. For filling, put prunes and water into a small saucepan. Bring to boiling. Reduce heat and simmer 10 to 15 minutes, or until mixture becomes mushy. Turn contents of saucepan into an electric blender container. Add the spices, lemon juice, honey, and brown sugar; cover and blend until smooth. Pour into a bowl and mix in sliced almonds. Cool.
2. For dough, soften yeast in warm water in a large bowl. Add oil, honey, salt, and milk. Stir in 1 cup whole wheat flour and chopped almonds. Beat vigorously 2 minutes. Beat in enough of the remaining flour to make a stiff dough.
3. Turn dough onto a surface lightly floured with whole wheat flour. Knead about 10 minutes, or until dough is smooth, elastic, and shows small blisters under surface when drawn tight.
4. Form dough into a ball and put into a greased deep bowl; turn to bring greased surface to top. Cover; let rise in a warm place until double in bulk (about 1¼ hours).
5. Punch dough down and turn onto a lightly floured surface. Divide in half. Roll each half into a 12×4-inch rectangle. Spread with half of cooled filling. Roll up jelly-roll fashion, starting with a 12-inch side, and shape into a half circle. Place seam side down on greased cookie sheet. Cut dough with kitchen scissors at 1-inch intervals about three quarters of the way through roll. Turn each section on its side. Cover and let rise again until double in bulk (about 45 minutes).
6. Bake at 425°F 10 minutes. Reduce to 350°F and bake 20 to 25 minutes.
7. Remove from oven and place on wire racks. If desired, sift confectioners' sugar over coffee cakes.

2 coffee cakes

Blueberry Pinwheel Rolls

- 2 cups all-purpose biscuit mix
- 2 tablespoons sugar
- 2 teaspoons grated orange peel
- ½ cup plus 2 tablespoons milk
- ¼ cup butter or margarine, melted
- ⅓ cup firmly packed brown sugar
- ½ teaspoon ground cinnamon
- ⅓ cup chopped pecans
- 1 cup fresh blueberries, rinsed and drained

1. Combine biscuit mix, sugar, and orange peel in a bowl. Add milk; stir with a fork until a dough is formed.
2. Turn dough onto a lightly floured surface. Shape into a ball and knead until dough is smooth. Roll dough into a rectangle, 18×10 inches. Brush dough with melted butter. Mix brown sugar, cinnamon, pecans, and blueberries and spoon over dough. Roll up jelly-roll fashion and cut into 12 equal pieces.
3. Put each piece cut side up into a well-greased muffin-pan well or paper baking-cup-lined muffin-pan well.
4. Bake at 425°F 15 to 20 minutes. Remove from muffin pans. Serve warm.

1 dozen rolls

Sandwiches and Snacks

Tired of the limp bologna sandwich routine? Try something new for a change. The sandwiches and snacks in this section combine good eating with nutritious ingredients from the basic Four Food Groups. Milk and cheese products are valued for their calcium, protein, and vitamin A content. The foods from the meat group that star in many of these recipes supply protein, iron, and B vitamins.

Cereal products such as breads and crackers provide B vitamins and iron. Fruits and vegetables are important sources of vitamins and minerals. Cheese, eggs, meat, fish, poultry, breads, crackers, fruits, and vegetables—each recipe is a mix-and-match combination of many of these ingredients. Nutrition-wise cooks will enjoy finding occasions to serve these tempting snacks and sandwiches.

Canadian-Mushroom Sandwiches

6 enriched kaiser rolls
   Butter or margarine, softened
1 tablespoon chopped uncooked
   bacon
2 tablespoons chopped onion
1 jar (2 ounces) sliced mushrooms,
   drained
1 teaspoon snipped parsley
18 slices (about 1 pound)
   Canadian-style bacon, cut ⅛
   inch thick
6 slices (1 ounce each) Swiss cheese
6 thin green pepper rings
   Paprika
   Cherry tomatoes
   Pimento-stuffed olives

1. Split rolls; if desired, reserve tops to accompany open-faced sandwiches. Spread roll bottoms with butter.
2. Combine bacon, onion, mushrooms, and parsley in a skillet and cook about 5 minutes.
3. Arrange 3 slices Canadian-style bacon on each buttered roll and top with mushroom mixture and 1 slice cheese. Place 1 green pepper ring on each cheese slice; sprinkle paprika inside ring.
4. Place sandwiches on a cookie sheet and broil 6 inches from heat until cheese melts (3 to 5 minutes). Garnish each with a cherry tomato and an olive on a skewer.

6 open-faced sandwiches

Hot Flank Steak Sandwiches

¼ cup olive oil
¼ cup red wine vinegar
2 cloves garlic, crushed in a garlic press or minced
6 peppercorns, crushed
½ teaspoon salt
½ teaspoon sugar
½ teaspoon chili powder
1 flank steak (about 1¼ pounds), scored
¼ cup butter or margarine
1 large sweet onion, thinly sliced
6 slices rye bread with caraway seed, or dark rye, toasted
1 can beef gravy, heated
Fresh parsley, finely snipped

1. Combine olive oil, vinegar, garlic, peppercorns, salt, sugar, and chili powder. Beat or shake to blend. Pour marinade over flank steak in a shallow dish. Cover and marinate in refrigerator at least 4 hours, turning meat occasionally.
2. Remove meat from marinade and place on broiler rack. Broil about 3 inches from heat 4 to 5 minutes on each side, or until desired degree of doneness; turn once.
3. Meanwhile, heat butter in a skillet and add onion; cook about 5 minutes, stirring occasionally.
4. Thinly slice meat diagonally across the grain. Place on toasted bread. Cover with cooked onion and spoon hot gravy over all. Garnish top with parsley. Serve immediately.

6 servings

Wonderful Western Heroes

4 brown-and-serve style enriched French rolls
2 cans (4½ ounces each) deviled ham
8 eggs
¼ cup milk
½ teaspoon seasoned salt
½ teaspoon crushed thyme
¼ cup minced onion
¼ cup minced green pepper
1 teaspoon vegetable oil
Onion rings
Green pepper rings

1. Bake rolls following package directions. Split into halves lengthwise; spread cut sides with deviled ham. Keep rolls warm.
2. Meanwhile, using a fork or rotary beater, mix eggs, milk, seasoned salt, and thyme in a bowl. Stir in onion and green pepper.
3. Heat oil in a 10-inch skillet over medium heat and pour in egg mixture. As mixture thickens, lift with fork or spatula from bottom and sides of skillet, allowing uncooked portion to flow to bottom; do not stir. When bottom is browned, cut egg mixture into four strips and turn each strip. Cook until browned.
4. Cut each egg strip in half and place each half strip on a roll half. Top each sandwich with onion and green pepper rings. Serve hot.

8 open-faced sandwiches

Saucy Beef 'n' Buns

2 tablespoons fat
½ cup finely chopped onion
1 pound ground beef
1 teaspoon salt
¼ teaspoon ground black pepper
¾ cup chopped celery
¾ cup chopped green pepper
1 cup chili sauce
1 cup ketchup
Enriched hamburger buns, buttered and toasted

1. Heat fat in a large skillet. Add onion and cook until soft, stirring occasionally. Add beef, salt, and pepper; cook until meat is lightly browned, separating it into pieces with a fork or spoon.
2. Add celery, green pepper, chili sauce, and ketchup; mix well. Simmer, uncovered, about 25 minutes; stir frequently.
3. To serve, spoon over toasted buns.

About 6 servings

Chickpea Salad Sandwiches

12 slices whole wheat bread
Butter or margarine
1 can (15½ ounces) chickpeas
(garbanzos), drained and
chopped
⅓ cup chopped green onion
3 tablespoons mayonnaise
1 tablespoon lemon juice
1½ teaspoons dried basil leaves,
crushed
½ teaspoon salt
⅛ teaspoon ground black pepper
6 lettuce leaves
1 can (16 ounces) bean sprouts,
drained
12 tomato slices
Seasoned salt, seasoned pepper, or
lemon pepper marinade
Carrot curls

1. Spread bread slices with butter.
2. Combine chickpeas, green onion, mayonnaise, lemon juice, basil, salt, and pepper in a bowl.
3. Place lettuce leaves on buttered side of 6 slices of bread. Top evenly with chickpea mixture and bean sprouts. Sprinkle sprouts and tomato slices with desired seasoning. Place 2 tomato slices on top and close sandwiches. Cut diagonally in half.
4. Garnish with carrot curls.

6 sandwiches

Turkey in Buns

¾ cup ketchup
1 cup currant jelly
¼ cup finely chopped onion
2 tablespoons Worcestershire sauce
1 teaspoon salt
¼ teaspoon garlic salt
3 cups diced cooked turkey
Enriched buns, split, buttered, and
toasted

1. Combine ketchup, jelly, onion, Worcestershire sauce, salt, and garlic salt in a saucepan. Set over low heat and bring to boiling, stirring occasionally. Reduce heat and simmer about 20 minutes. Stir in turkey. Heat thoroughly.
2. Spoon turkey mixture into buns.

8 to 10 servings

The Apple Special

12 slices enriched white sandwich
bread
Mayonnaise or salad dressing
Prepared mustard
12 slices (1 ounce each) cooked ham
36 to 48 slices apple (such as
Jonathan or McIntosh), pared,
if desired
24 slices (1 ounce each) pasteurized
process American cheese

1. Spread bread slices lightly with mayonnaise, then with prepared mustard. Cover each slice with 1 slice ham, 3 or 4 slices apple, and 2 slices cheese.
2. Place sandwiches on cookie sheet and broil 4 inches from heat until cheese is lightly browned (about 3 minutes). Serve hot.

12 open-faced sandwiches

Note: If desired, toast bread on one side, turn, and spread untoasted side.

Chicken Fiesta Buns

3 tablespoons butter or margarine
⅓ cup finely chopped green pepper
⅓ cup finely chopped celery
⅓ cup finely chopped onion
1 clove garlic, minced
½ cup tomato paste
2 tablespoons Worcestershire sauce
2 tablespoons cider vinegar
1 tablespoon brown sugar
½ teaspoon chili powder
½ teaspoon salt
¼ teaspoon seasoned pepper
1½ cups chopped cooked chicken or turkey
¼ cup chopped pimento-stuffed olives
8 enriched frankfurter buns, split and heated

1. Heat butter in a skillet and add green pepper, celery, onion, and garlic; cook about 3 minutes.
2. Mix tomato paste, Worcestershire sauce, vinegar, brown sugar, chili powder, salt, and seasoned pepper. Add to skillet along with chicken and olives; stir well. Bring to boiling, reduce heat, and simmer about 10 minutes to blend flavors, stirring occasionally.
3. To serve, spoon hot chicken mixture into buns.

8 servings

Scrumptious Tunaburgers

2 eggs
¼ cup ketchup
1 tablespoon lemon juice
2 tablespoons capers
2 teaspoons instant minced onion
¾ teaspoon lemon pepper marinade
1½ cups soft enriched bread crumbs
3 cans (6½ or 7 ounces each) tuna, drained and flaked
2 tablespoons butter or margarine
6 enriched hamburger buns, halved, buttered, and toasted

1. Beat eggs slightly in a bowl. Add ketchup, lemon juice, capers, onion, lemon pepper marinade, bread crumbs, and tuna; mix thoroughly.
2. Heat butter in a large skillet.
3. Meanwhile, shape tuna mixture into 6 patties (mixture will not be smooth). Put patties into hot butter as each is shaped. Cook over medium heat until browned. Using a large spatula, carefully turn patties to brown other side. Immediately transfer to toasted buns.

6 burgers

Note: If desired, serve tunaburgers with any of the following: ketchup, sweet onion slices, avocado wedges, tomato slices, green pepper rings, cucumber spears, lemon wedges, Cheddar or Swiss cheese slices.

Cream Cheese-Peanut Sandwich Filling

1 package (8 ounces) cream cheese, softened
2 to 3 tablespoons milk or cream
¼ teaspoon instant minced onion
2 or 3 drops Tabasco
¼ teaspoon Worcestershire sauce
¼ cup Spanish peanuts, chopped
¼ cup chopped pimento-stuffed olives

Combine cream cheese, milk, onion, Tabasco, and Worcestershire sauce in a small bowl. Beat with an electric beater until the consistency of whipped cream, adding more milk, if necessary. Stir in peanuts and olives.

About 1½ cups filling

Note: If desired, substitute ¼ cup chopped ripe olives for the stuffed olives and mix in 2 to 4 tablespoons flaked coconut.

Pork Loin Roast, 40;
Hash Brown Potatoes au Gratin, 68

Fruit-Cottage Cheese Sandwich Filling

1 cup creamed cottage cheese
¼ cup pitted dates, finely snipped
¼ cup raisins, finely snipped
⅛ teaspoon salt

Combine cottage cheese, dates, raisins, and salt in a bowl; mix well. Chill thoroughly. Stir before using.

About 1½ cups filling

Cheddar-Stuffed Celery

1 teaspoon dry mustard
6 tablespoons cream
2 tablespoons dairy sour cream
1 tablespoon minced onion
½ teaspoon Worcestershire sauce
¼ teaspoon seasoned salt
1 small clove garlic, crushed in a garlic press
2 cups (8 ounces) shredded very sharp Cheddar cheese
Crisp celery, cut in diagonal lengths, rinsed, dried, and chilled

1. Measure dry mustard into a bowl and gradually add cream, stirring until mustard is diluted. Blend in sour cream, onion, Worcestershire sauce, seasoned salt, and garlic. Using an electric hand mixer, add cheese gradually, beating until blended.
2. Stuff celery lengths.

About 1½ cups cheese stuffing for celery

Note: Mixture may be used as an appetizer spread for crackers and toasted cocktail rye bread slices. Or, thin with additional cream or sour cream for a cheese dip.

Spinach Crescents

1 package refrigerated fresh dough for crescent rolls
Italian salad dressing
Grated Parmesan-Romano cheese
1 cup finely snipped fresh spinach
5 tablespoons prepared baconlike pieces (a soy protein product)

1. Divide roll dough into triangles; cut each lengthwise in half. Brush dough with Italian salad dressing. Sprinkle with grated cheese. Mix spinach and baconlike pieces; spoon over triangles and press into dough. Roll up and place on a cookie sheet, curving to form crescents.
2. Bake at 375°F 10 to 15 minutes.

16 rolls

Favorite Salmon Sandwich Filling

¾ cup flaked canned salmon
½ cup finely chopped cabbage
3 tablespoons chopped ripe olives
1 tablespoon olive liquid
¼ teaspoon paprika
2 or 3 drops Tabasco
3 tablespoons mayonnaise or salad dressing

Put salmon, cabbage, and ripe olives into a bowl. Add olive liquid, paprika, Tabasco, and mayonnaise; mix well.

About 1½ cups filling

Chicken and Dumplings, 44

Apricot-Nut Chews

1 cup dried apricots
1 cup pitted dates or dried figs
(stems removed)
1 cup raisins
½ cup almonds or walnuts, chopped
½ cup maple-blended syrup
⅛ teaspoon salt
Coconut, flaked or finely chopped
Finely chopped nuts

1. Put apricots and dates through coarse blade of food chopper. Mix and grind once more. Put into top of double boiler with raisins, almonds, syrup, and salt. Cook over boiling water until fruit softens slightly. Stir until well blended. Set aside to cool.
2. Shape mixture into balls, about 1¼ inches in diameter. Roll some in coconut and some in nuts.
3. To store, wrap in waxed paper and keep in a cool place.

About 2 dozen balls

Rumaki

½ pound chicken livers
1½ tablespoons honey
1 tablespoon soy sauce
2 tablespoons vegetable oil
½ clove garlic, crushed in a garlic press
1 can (5 ounces) water chestnuts, drained and cut in quarters
Bacon slices, cut in halves or thirds

1. Rinse chicken livers with running cold water and drain on absorbent paper; cut into halves and put into a bowl.
2. Pour a mixture of honey, soy sauce, oil, and garlic over the liver pieces. Cover. Let stand about 30 minutes, turning pieces occasionally. Remove from marinade and set aside on absorbent paper to drain.
3. Wrap a piece of bacon around a twosome of liver and water chestnut pieces, threading each onto a wooden pick or small skewer.
4. Put appetizers on rack in broiler pan with top of appetizers about 3 inches from heat and broil about 5 minutes. Turn with tongs and broil until bacon is browned. Serve hot.

About 1½ dozen appetizers

Shrimp Cocktail Seviche Style

1½ pounds cooked shrimp, shelled, deveined, and chilled
1 firm ripe tomato, peeled and diced
¼ cup thinly sliced green onions with tops
¼ cup thinly sliced celery
½ cup lime juice
1½ teaspoons salt
2 to 3 teaspoons soy sauce
¼ teaspoon Worcestershire sauce
½ clove garlic, minced
Leaf lettuce

1. Dice chilled shrimp into a bowl and combine with tomato, green onion, celery, lime juice, salt, soy sauce, Worcestershire sauce, and garlic; toss lightly to mix well. Chill, covered, about 8 hours, or overnight.
2. Serve very cold on cocktail sea shells lined with leaf lettuce.

6 servings

Meat

In most homes a meat dish is the main attraction at dinner. Nutritionally speaking, meat well deserves to be the center of attention at mealtime, as it is an important source of protein and iron. Thiamine, riboflavin, and niacin are also found in meats. Numerous meat dishes achieve their special character in combination with fruits and vegetables, which are valuable sources of additional nutrients, especially vitamins.

Many of the following recipes dress up traditional stand-bys as never before. Working people will appreciate the many quickly prepared meat dishes in this section. Do-aheads, in particular, are real timesavers.

Meat purchases are likely to take a sizable portion of the weekly food budget, but these recipes make it possible to prepare meals that are convenient, healthful, and economical.

Italian-Style Meat Stew

¼ cup olive oil
1 pound lean beef for stew (1½-inch cubes)
1 pound lean lamb for stew (1½-inch cubes)
1 can (28 ounces) tomatoes (undrained)
1½ cups boiling water
1½ cups chopped onion
1 cup diced celery
2 teaspoons salt
½ teaspoon ground black pepper
4 large potatoes, pared and quartered (about 3 cups)
5 large carrots, pared and cut in strips (about 2 cups)
1 teaspoon basil, crushed
¼ teaspoon garlic powder
½ cup cold water
¼ cup enriched all-purpose flour

1. Heat oil in a large saucepot or Dutch oven; add meat and brown on all sides.
2. Add undrained tomatoes, boiling water, onion, celery, salt, and pepper to saucepot. Cover and simmer 1 to 1½ hours, or until meat is almost tender.
3. Add potatoes, carrots, basil, and garlic powder to saucepot; mix well. Simmer 45 minutes, or until meat and vegetables are tender when pierced with a fork.
4. Blend cold water and flour; add gradually to meat-and-vegetable mixture, stirring constantly. Bring to boiling and continue to stir and boil 1 to 2 minutes, or until sauce is thickened. (Leftover sauce may be served the following day on mashed potatoes.)

8 to 10 servings

Oxtail Stew

½ cup enriched all-purpose flour
1 teaspoon salt
¼ teaspoon ground black pepper
3 oxtails (about 1 pound each), disjointed
3 tablespoons butter or margarine
1½ cups chopped onion
1 can (28 ounces) tomatoes, drained (reserve liquid)
1½ cups hot water
4 medium potatoes, pared
6 medium carrots, pared
2 pounds fresh peas, shelled
1 tablespoon paprika
1 teaspoon salt
¼ teaspoon ground black pepper
¼ cup cold water
2 tablespoons flour

1. Mix ½ cup flour, 1 teaspoon salt, and ¼ teaspoon pepper in a plastic bag; coat oxtail pieces evenly by shaking two or three at a time.
2. Heat butter in a 3-quart top-of-range casserole. Add onion and cook until soft. Remove onion with a slotted spoon and set aside.
3. Put meat into casserole and brown on all sides. Return onion to casserole. Pour in the reserved tomato liquid (set tomatoes aside) and hot water. Cover tightly and simmer 2½ to 3 hours, or until meat is almost tender when pierced with a fork.
4. When meat has cooked about 2 hours, cut potatoes and carrots into small balls, using a melon-ball cutter. Cut the tomatoes into pieces.
5. When meat is almost tender, mix in potatoes, carrots, peas, paprika, 1 teaspoon salt, and ¼ teaspoon pepper. Cover and simmer 20 minutes. Stir in tomatoes and cook 10 minutes, or until meat and vegetables are tender. Put meat and vegetables into a warm dish.
6. Blend cold water and 2 tablespoons flour; add half gradually to cooking liquid, stirring constantly. Bring to boiling; gradually add only what is needed of remaining flour mixture for desired gravy consistency. Bring to boiling after each addition. Cook 3 to 5 minutes after final addition. Return meat and vegetables to casserole and heat thoroughly.

6 to 8 servings

Sauerbraten Moderne

1 cup wine vinegar
1 cup water
1 medium onion, thinly sliced
2 tablespoons sugar
1 teaspoon salt
5 peppercorns
3 whole cloves
1 bay leaf
2 pounds beef round steak (¾ inch thick), boneless, cut in cubes
1 lemon, thinly sliced
2 tablespoons butter or margarine
1 can (10¾ ounces) beef gravy
1 can (3 ounces) broiled sliced mushrooms (undrained)
6 gingersnaps, crumbled (about ⅔ cup)
Cooked noodles

1. Combine vinegar, water, onion, sugar, salt, peppercorns, cloves, and bay leaf in a saucepan. Heat just to boiling.
2. Meanwhile, put meat into a large shallow dish and arrange lemon slices over it. Pour hot vinegar mixture into dish. Cover and allow to marinate about 2 hours.
3. Remove and discard peppercorns, cloves, bay leaf, and lemon slices; reserve onion. Drain meat thoroughly, reserving marinade.
4. Heat butter in a skillet over medium heat. Add meat and brown pieces on all sides. Stir 1 cup of the reserved liquid with the onion into skillet. Cover, bring to boiling, reduce heat, and simmer about 45 minutes.
5. Blend beef gravy and mushrooms with liquid into mixture in skillet. Bring to boiling and simmer, loosely covered, about 20 minutes longer, or until meat is tender.
6. Add the crumbled gingersnaps to mixture in skillet and cook, stirring constantly, until gravy is thickened. Serve over noodles.

6 to 8 servings

Company Beef and Peaches

1 can (8 ounces) tomato sauce with
    onions
1 can (8 ounces) sliced peaches,
    drained; reserve syrup
¾ cup beef broth
2 tablespoons brown sugar
2 tablespoons lemon juice
1 tablespoon prepared mustard
1 teaspoon Worcestershire sauce
1 clove garlic, minced
1 beef round bottom round roast or
    eye round roast, boneless (2 to 3
    pounds)
  Vegetable oil
  Salt and seasoned pepper
2 tablespoons cold water
2 teaspoons cornstarch
  Watercress or parsley

1. Turn the tomato sauce with onions into a bowl. Mix in the peach syrup (set peaches aside), beef broth, brown sugar, lemon juice, prepared mustard, Worcestershire sauce, and garlic. Set aside.
2. Cut meat across the grain into 6 to 8 slices, about ¾ inch thick.
3. Heat oil in a large skillet. Add the meat slices and brown on both sides. Sprinkle with salt and seasoned pepper. Pour the sauce mixture over the meat. Bring to boiling, reduce heat, and simmer, covered, about 1½ hours, or until meat is fork-tender; turn meat slices occasionally.
4. Overlap meat slices to one side of a heated serving platter.
5. Blend water and cornstarch; stir into sauce in skillet. Bring to boiling; cook about 1 minute. Mix in sliced peaches and heat thoroughly; spoon to the side of meat on the platter. Cover meat with sauce. Garnish with watercress.

6 to 8 servings

Red-Topper Meat Loaf

Meat loaf:
2 tablespoons butter or margarine
¾ cup finely chopped onion
¼ cup chopped green pepper
1½ pounds lean ground beef
½ pound bulk pork sausage
1 cup uncooked oats, quick or old
    fashioned
2 eggs, beaten
¾ cup tomato juice
¼ cup prepared horseradish
2 teaspoons salt
1 teaspoon dry mustard
½ teaspoon monosodium glutamate

Topping:
1 to 3 tablespoons brown sugar
1 teaspoon dry mustard
¼ cup ketchup

1. For meat loaf, heat butter in a skillet. Mix in onion and green pepper; cook about 5 minutes, or until onion is soft.
2. Meanwhile, lightly mix beef, sausage, and oats in a large bowl. Combine eggs, tomato juice, horseradish, salt, dry mustard, and monosodium glutamate; add to meat mixture and mix lightly. Turn into a 9×5×3-inch loaf pan and press lightly.
3. For topping, mix brown sugar with dry mustard and blend in ketchup. Spread over meat loaf.
4. Bake at 375°F about 1 hour. Remove from oven and allow meat to stand several minutes before slicing.

About 8 servings

Liver-Apple Bake

1 pound sliced beef liver (about ¼
    inch thick)
2 cups chopped apple
½ cup chopped onion
2 teaspoons seasoned salt
⅛ teaspoon ground black pepper
4 slices bacon, cut in thirds
  Parsley sprigs

1. Remove tubes and outer membrane from liver, if necessary. Put liver slices into a greased shallow baking dish.
2. Combine apple, onion, seasoned salt, and pepper; toss to mix. Spoon over liver. Arrange bacon pieces over top. Cover dish.
3. Cook in a 325°F oven 1 hour. Remove cover and continue cooking about 15 minutes.
4. Garnish with parsley.

4 servings

Short Ribs, Western Style

4 medium onions, peeled and
   quartered
2 teaspoons salt
¼ teaspoon ground black pepper
½ teaspoon rubbed sage
1 quart water
1 cup dried lima beans
3 tablespoons flour
1 teaspoon dry mustard
2 to 3 tablespoons fat
2 pounds beef rib short ribs, cut in
   serving-size pieces

1. Combine onions, salt, pepper, sage, and water in a large heavy saucepot or Dutch oven. Cover, bring to boiling, reduce heat, and simmer 5 minutes. Bring to boiling again; add lima beans gradually and cook, uncovered, 2 minutes. Remove from heat, cover, and set aside to soak 1 hour.
2. Meanwhile, mix flour and dry mustard and coat short ribs evenly.
3. Heat fat in a large heavy skillet and brown short ribs on all sides over medium heat. Add meat to soaked lima beans. Bring to boiling and simmer, covered, 1½ hours, or until beans and meat are tender.

About 6 servings

Kidney Bean Rice Olympian

2 tablespoons olive oil
1½ pounds beef round steak,
   boneless, cut in 1-inch cubes
2 teaspoons salt
¼ teaspoon ground black pepper
2 large cloves garlic, crushed in a
   garlic press
2 cups beef broth
1 cup sliced celery
1 can (16 ounces) tomatoes, cut in
   pieces (undrained)
2 cans (16 ounces each) kidney
   beans (undrained)
1 large green pepper, diced
3 cups hot cooked rice
1 large head lettuce, finely shredded
3 medium onions, peeled and
   coarsely chopped

1. Heat olive oil in a large heavy skillet. Add meat and brown on all sides. Add salt, pepper, and garlic; pour in beef broth. Bring to boiling, reduce heat, and simmer, covered, about 1 hour.
2. Stir celery and tomatoes and beans with liquid into beef in skillet; bring to boiling and simmer, covered, 30 minutes. Add green pepper and continue cooking 30 minutes.
3. To serve, spoon rice onto each serving plate, cover generously with shredded lettuce, and spoon a generous portion of the bean mixture over lettuce. Top each serving with about 3 tablespoons chopped onion.

About 8 servings

Lamb Crown Roast with Mint Stuffing

8 slices enriched white bread,
   toasted and cubed
1 unpared red apple, cored and
   diced
1½ tablespoons coarsely chopped
   mint or 1½ teaspoons dried
   mint flakes
¾ teaspoon poultry seasoning

1. Combine toasted bread cubes, apple, mint, poultry seasoning, and salt in a large bowl.
2. Heat butter in a saucepan. Mix in celery and onion and cook about 5 minutes. Pour over bread mixture along with water; toss lightly.
3. Place lamb on a rack, rib ends up, in a shallow roasting pan. Fill center with stuffing.
4. Roast in a 325°F oven about 2½ hours, or until a meat

½ teaspoon salt
6 tablespoons butter
½ cup chopped celery
¼ cup chopped onion
½ cup water
1 lamb rib crown roast (5 to 6 pounds)

thermometer registers 175° to 180°F (depending on desired degree of doneness).

5. Place roast on a heated serving platter. Prepare gravy, if desired. Accompany with Parsley-Buttered New Potatoes (page 68) and Butter-Sauced Asparagus (page 65).

About 8 servings

Lamb Kabobs

1½ pounds lamb (leg, loin, or shoulder), boneless, cut in 1½-inch cubes
½ cup vegetable oil
1 tablespoon lemon juice
2 teaspoons sugar
½ teaspoon salt
½ teaspoon paprika
¼ teaspoon dry mustard
⅛ teaspoon ground black pepper
¼ teaspoon Worcestershire sauce
1 clove garlic, cut in halves
6 small whole cooked potatoes
6 small whole cooked onions
Butter or margarine, melted
6 plum tomatoes

1. Put lamb cubes into a shallow dish. Combine oil, lemon juice, sugar, salt, paprika, dry mustard, pepper, Worcestershire sauce, and garlic. Pour over meat. Cover and marinate at least 1 hour in refrigerator, turning pieces occasionally. Drain.

2. Alternately thread lamb cubes, potatoes, and onions on 6 skewers. Brush pieces with melted butter.

3. Broil 3 to 4 inches from heat about 15 minutes, or until lamb is desired degree of doneness; turn frequently and brush with melted butter. Shortly before kabobs are done, impale tomatoes on ends of skewers.

6 servings

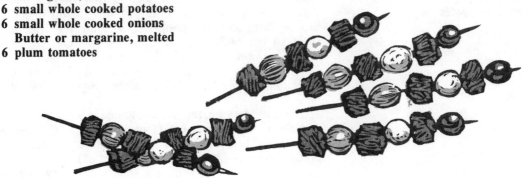

Oven Lamb Stew

2 pounds lean lamb shoulder, boneless, cut in 2-inch cubes
1¾ teaspoons salt
¼ teaspoon thyme, crushed
1 bay leaf
4 whole allspice
2 tablespoons chopped parsley
1 clove garlic, minced
¼ small head cabbage, shredded
2 leeks, thinly sliced
2 medium onions, sliced
1 cup sliced raw potatoes
4 cups water
8 small onions
4 carrots, cut in 2-inch pieces
2 white turnips, quartered

1. Put lamb into a Dutch oven. Season with salt, thyme, bay leaf, allspice, parsley, and garlic. Add cabbage, leeks, sliced onions, and potatoes. Pour in water. Cover tightly and bring rapidly to boiling.

2. Cook in a 350°F oven about 1½ hours, or until meat is tender.

3. About 30 minutes before cooking time is ended, cook whole onions, carrots, and turnips separately in boiling salted water until tender. Drain.

4. Turn contents of Dutch oven into a food mill set over a large bowl. Return meat to the Dutch oven and add the cooked onions, carrots, and turnips. Discard bay leaf and allspice; force the vegetables through food mill into the bowl containing cooking liquid (or purée vegetables in an electric blender). Heat with meat and vegetables.

6 to 8 servings

Roast Leg of Lamb

- 1 teaspoon salt
- ½ teaspoon monosodium glutamate
- ½ teaspoon ground black pepper
- 1 teaspoon seasoned salt
- ½ teaspoon ground marjoram
- ¼ teaspoon dry mustard
- ⅛ teaspoon ground cardamom
- 1 lamb leg, whole (about 6 pounds)
- 2 cloves garlic, cut in slivers
- ½ teaspoon ground thyme
  - Orange peel, cut in slivers
  - Fresh mint sprigs (optional)

1. Mix salt, monosodium glutamate, pepper, seasoned salt, marjoram, dry mustard, and cardamom; rub over lamb. Cut about 16 deep slits in roast. Toss garlic and thyme together. Insert garlic in each slit along with a sliver of orange peel.
2. Place lamb, fat side up, on a rack in a shallow roasting pan. Insert meat thermometer in center of thickest portion of meat.
3. Roast, uncovered, in a 325°F oven 2½ to 3 hours. Meat is medium done when thermometer registers 175°F and is well done at 180°F.
4. Remove meat thermometer. Place roast on a warm serving platter. Put a paper frill around end of leg bone and garnish platter with mint, if desired.

About 10 servings

Pork Loin Roast

- 1 pork loin roast (4 to 6 pounds)
  - Salt and pepper
  - Spiced crab apples

1. Have the meat retailer saw across the rib bones of roast at base of the backbone, separating the ribs from the backbone. Place roast, fat side up, on a rack in an open roasting pan. Season with salt and pepper. Insert meat thermometer in roast so the bulb is centered in the thickest part and not resting on bone or in fat.
2. Roast in a 350°F oven about 2½ to 3 hours, or until thermometer registers 170°F; allow 30 to 40 minutes per pound.
3. For easy carving, remove backbone, place roast on platter, and allow roast to set for 15 to 20 minutes. Garnish platter with spiced crab apples, heated if desired. Accompany with Hash Brown Potatoes au Gratin (page 68).

8 to 10 servings

Veal Glacé

- 1 cup dry white wine
- 1½ teaspoons tarragon leaves
- 1½ pounds veal cutlets (about ¼ inch thick)
- 3 tablespoons butter
- ½ teaspoon salt
- ⅛ teaspoon ground black pepper
- ½ cup condensed consommé (undiluted)
- ½ cup dry vermouth

1. Stir tarragon into white wine. Cover; allow to stand several hours, stirring occasionally.
2. Cut meat into pieces about 3×2 inches. Heat butter in skillet until lightly browned. Add meat and brown lightly. Season with salt and pepper. Reduce heat and pour in tarragon wine mixture with the consommé and vermouth. Simmer uncovered, about 10 minutes, or until veal is tender.
3. Remove veal to a heated dish and cover. Increase heat under skillet and cook sauce until it is reduced to a thin glaze (about 10 minutes), stirring occasionally.
4. Pour glaze over meat, turning meat to coat evenly. Serve hot.

About 6 servings

Note: If desired, accompany with buttered fluffy rice tossed with chopped parsley and toasted slivered almonds.

Curried Veal and Vegetables

1 pound veal for stew (1-inch cubes)
2 cups water
1 teaspoon salt
3 medium carrots, pared and cut in quarters
½ pound green beans
2 large stalks celery, cut in ½-inch slices
3 tablespoons butter or margarine
2 tablespoons flour
½ teaspoon curry powder
¼ teaspoon salt
Cooked rice
Fresh parsley, snipped

1. Put veal into a large saucepan with water and 1 teaspoon salt. Cover, bring to boiling, reduce heat, and simmer 1 hour. Add carrots, green beans, and celery. Cover, bring to boiling, and simmer 1 hour, or until meat is tender.
2. Remove meat and vegetables from broth with a slotted spoon; set aside. Reserve broth.
3. Heat butter in a saucepan. Blend in flour, curry powder, and ¼ teaspoon salt. Heat until bubbly. Add reserved broth gradually, stirring until smooth. Bring to boiling, stirring constantly, and cook 1 to 2 minutes. Mix in meat and vegetables. Heat thoroughly.
4. Serve over rice. Sprinkle with parsley.

About 6 servings

Saucy Ham Loaf

Meat loaf:
1½ pounds ground cooked ham
½ pound ground veal
½ pound ground pork
2 eggs, fork beaten
½ teaspoon salt
⅛ teaspoon ground black pepper
½ teaspoon ground nutmeg
½ teaspoon dry mustard
¼ teaspoon ground thyme
¼ cup finely chopped onion
½ cup finely chopped green pepper
2 tablespoons finely chopped parsley
¾ cup soft enriched bread crumbs
¾ cup apple juice

Sauce:
⅔ cup packed light brown sugar
2 teaspoons cornstarch
1 teaspoon dry mustard
1 teaspoon ground allspice
⅔ cup apricot nectar
3 tablespoons lemon juice
2 teaspoons vinegar

1. Combine ham, veal, and pork with eggs, salt, pepper, nutmeg, dry mustard, and thyme in a large bowl. Add onion, green pepper, and parsley and toss to blend. Add bread crumbs and apple juice; mix thoroughly but lightly. Turn into a 9×5×3-inch loaf pan and flatten top.
2. Bake at 350°F 1 hour.
3. Meanwhile, prepare sauce for topping. Blend brown sugar, cornstarch, dry mustard, and allspice in a small saucepan. Add apricot nectar, lemon juice, and vinegar. Bring rapidly to boiling and cook about 2 minutes, stirring constantly. Reduce heat and simmer 10 minutes to allow flavors to blend.
4. Remove meat loaf from oven; pour off and reserve juices. Unmold loaf in a shallow baking pan. Spoon some of the reserved juices and then the sauce over loaf. Return to oven 30 minutes.
5. Place loaf on a warm platter and garnish as desired.

8 to 10 servings

Canadian-Style Bacon and Peaches

Roast Canadian-Style Bacon:
- 2 pounds smoked pork loin Canadian-style bacon (in one piece)
- 10 whole cloves

Orange-Spiced Peaches:
- ½ cup firmly packed brown sugar
- ⅓ cup red wine vinegar
- 1 tablespoon grated orange peel
- 2 tablespoons orange juice
- 1 teaspoon whole cloves
- ½ teaspoon whole allspice
- 1 can (29 ounces) peach halves, drained; reserve 1½ cups syrup
- Mustard Sauce

1. Remove casing from the meat and place, fat side up, on a rack in a shallow roasting pan. Stud with cloves. Insert a meat thermometer into bacon so bulb is centered. Roast, uncovered, at 325°F about 2 hours, or until thermometer registers 160°F.
2. For Orange-Spiced Peaches, stir brown sugar, wine vinegar, orange peel, orange juice, cloves, allspice, and peach syrup together in a saucepan. Bring to boiling; reduce heat and simmer 5 minutes. Mix in peaches and heat 5 minutes.
3. Remove from heat and allow peaches to cool in syrup. Refrigerate until ready to serve.
4. Shortly before meat is roasted, prepare Mustard Sauce.
5. Remove meat from oven and place on a heated serving platter. Remove thermometer. Arrange peaches on platter. Accompany with Mustard Sauce in a bowl.

About 8 servings

Mustard Sauce: Mix **1 cup firmly packed brown sugar, 2 tablespoons prepared mustard, 1 tablespoon butter or margarine, 3 tablespoons cider vinegar** in a saucepan. Stir over low heat until sugar is dissolved; heat thoroughly, stirring occasionally.

⅔ cup sauce

Savory Sweetbreads

- 1½ pounds sweetbreads
- Cold water
- ¼ cup lemon juice
- 1 teaspoon salt
- 1½ cups beef broth
- 2 stalks celery with leaves, cut in 1-inch pieces
- 2 sprigs parsley
- ¼ teaspoon savory
- ¼ teaspoon thyme
- ⅛ teaspoon ground allspice
- ⅛ teaspoon ground nutmeg
- ⅓ cup butter or margarine
- 2 tablespoons flour
- 2 teaspoons dry mustard
- 1 teaspoon monosodium glutamate
- ⅛ teaspoon ground black pepper
- 1 tablespoon vinegar
- ¼ cup coarsely snipped parsley
- Melba toast (optional)

1. Rinse sweetbreads with cold water as soon as possible after purchase. Put sweetbreads into a saucepan. Cover with cold water and add lemon juice and salt. Cover saucepan, bring to boiling, reduce heat, and simmer 20 minutes. Drain sweetbreads; cover with cold water. Drain again. (Cool and refrigerate if sweetbreads are not to be used immediately.) Remove tubes and membrane; reserve. Separate sweetbreads into smaller pieces and slice; set aside.
2. Pour broth into a saucepan. Add the tubes and membrane, celery, parsley, savory, thyme, allspice, and nutmeg. Bring to boiling and simmer, covered, 30 minutes. Strain broth, reserving 1 cup.
3. Heat butter in a skillet. Blend in flour, dry mustard, monosodium glutamate, and pepper. Heat until bubbly. Add the reserved broth and vinegar while stirring until smooth. Bring to boiling, stirring constantly, and cook until thickened. Add the sweetbreads and parsley. Heat thoroughly.
4. Serve over Melba toast, if desired.

About 6 servings

Poultry

Poultry dishes are popular around the world. Chicken in particular is an international favorite, and with the following recipes any cook can enjoy preparing chicken with a foreign flavor. There also are exciting new recipes for preparing turkey, duck, and goose.

Budget-conscious gourmets will enjoy serving a variety of poultry dishes often. Although prices tend to fluctuate, chicken and turkey are almost always economical buys.

Poultry is popular not only for its low cost and adaptability to many flavor combinations, but also because of its nutritional value. High in protein and low in fat, chicken and turkey are always welcome among weight watchers. They also contain niacin, iron, thiamine, and riboflavin.

Chicken, Cacciatore Style

¼ cup vegetable oil
1 broiler-fryer chicken (about 2½ pounds), cut in serving-size pieces
2 medium onions, sliced
2 cloves garlic, crushed in a garlic press or minced
3 tomatoes, sliced
2 medium green peppers, sliced
1 small bay leaf
1 teaspoon salt
¼ teaspoon ground black pepper
½ teaspoon celery seed
1 teaspoon crushed oregano or basil
1 can (8 ounces) tomato sauce
¼ cup sauterne
8 ounces spaghetti, cooked

1. Heat oil in a large heavy skillet. Add chicken and brown on all sides. Remove chicken from skillet.
2. Add onions and garlic to oil remaining in skillet and cook until onion is tender but not brown; stir occasionally to cook evenly.
3. Return chicken to skillet and add the tomatoes, green peppers, and bay leaf.
4. Mix salt, pepper, celery seed, and oregano with tomato sauce; pour over all.
5. Cover and cook over low heat 45 minutes. Blend in sauterne and cook, uncovered, 20 minutes. Discard bay leaf.
6. Put cooked spaghetti onto a warm serving platter and top with the chicken pieces and sauce.

About 6 servings

Chicken and Dumplings

¼ cup butter or margarine
2 broiler-fryer chickens, cut in serving-size pieces
½ cup chopped onion
¼ cup chopped celery
2 tablespoons chopped celery leaves
1 clove garlic, minced
¼ cup enriched all-purpose flour
4 cups chicken broth
1 teaspoon sugar
2 teaspoons salt
¼ teaspoon ground black pepper
1 teaspoon basil leaves
2 bay leaves
¼ cup chopped parsley
   Basil Dumplings
2 packages (10 ounces each) frozen green peas

1. Heat butter in a large skillet. Add chicken pieces and brown on all sides. Remove chicken from skillet.
2. Add onion, celery, celery leaves, and garlic to fat in skillet. Cook until vegetables are tender. Sprinkle with flour and mix well. Add chicken broth, sugar, salt, pepper, basil, bay leaves, and parsley; bring to boiling, stirring constantly. Return chicken to skillet and spoon sauce over it; cover.
3. Cook in a 350°F oven 40 minutes.
4. Shortly before cooking time is completed, prepare Basil Dumplings.
5. Remove skillet from oven and turn control to 425°F. Stir peas into skillet mixture and bring to boiling. Drop dumpling dough onto stew.
6. Return to oven and cook, uncovered, 10 minutes; cover and cook 10 minutes, or until chicken is tender and dumplings are done.

About 8 servings

Basil Dumplings: Combine **2 cups all-purpose biscuit mix** and **1 teaspoon basil leaves** in a bowl. Add **⅔ cup milk** and stir with a fork until a dough is formed. Proceed as directed in recipe.

Chicken Fricassee with Vegetables

1 broiler-fryer chicken (about 3 pounds), cut in serving-size pieces
1½ teaspoons salt
1 bay leaf
   Water
2 cups sliced carrots
2 onions, quartered
2 crookneck squashes, cut in halves lengthwise
2 pattypan squashes, cut in halves
   Green beans (about 6 ounces), tips cut off
1 can (3½ ounces) pitted ripe olives, drained
1 tablespoon cornstarch
2 tablespoons water

1. Place chicken pieces along with salt and bay leaf in a Dutch oven or saucepot. Add enough water to just cover chicken. Bring to boiling; simmer, covered, 25 minutes until chicken is almost tender.
2. Add carrots and onions to cooking liquid; cook, covered, 10 minutes. Add squashes and green beans to cooking liquid; cook, covered, 10 minutes, or until chicken and vegetables are tender. Remove chicken and vegetables to a warm serving dish and add olives; keep hot.
3. Blend cornstarch and 2 tablespoons water; stir into boiling cooking liquid. Boil 2 to 3 minutes. Pour gravy over chicken.

About 4 servings

Chicken Polynesian Style

2 cups chicken broth
1 package (10 ounces) frozen mixed
    vegetables
½ cup diagonally sliced celery
1½ tablespoons cornstarch
1 teaspoon monosodium glutamate
½ teaspoon sugar
½ teaspoon seasoned salt
⅛ teaspoon ground black pepper
½ teaspoon Worcestershire sauce
1 small clove garlic, minced or
    crushed in a garlic press
1 tablespoon instant minced onion
1 can (6 ounces) ripe olives, drained
    and cut in wedges
    Cooked chicken, cut in 1-inch
    pieces (about 2 cups)
    Chow mein noodles
    Salted peanuts
    Soy sauce

1. Heat ½ cup chicken broth in a saucepan. Add frozen vegetables and celery; cook, covered, until crisp-tender. Remove vegetables and set aside; reserve any cooking liquid in saucepan.
2. Mix cornstarch, monosodium glutamate, sugar, seasoned salt, and pepper; blend with ¼ cup of the chicken broth. Add remaining broth, Worcestershire sauce, garlic, and onion to the saucepan. Add cornstarch mixture; bring to boiling, stirring constantly. Cook and stir 2 to 3 minutes.
3. Mix in olives, chicken, and reserved vegetables; heat thoroughly, stirring occasionally.
4. Serve over chow mein noodles and top generously with peanuts. Accompany with a cruet of soy sauce.

About 6 servings

Country Captain

1 broiler-fryer chicken (3 to 3½
    pounds), cut in serving-size
    pieces
¼ cup enriched all-purpose flour
½ teaspoon salt
    Pinch ground white pepper
3 to 4 tablespoons lard
2 onions, finely chopped
2 medium green peppers, chopped
1 clove garlic, crushed in a garlic
    press or minced
1½ teaspoons salt
½ teaspoon ground white pepper
1½ teaspoons curry powder
½ teaspoon ground thyme
½ teaspoon snipped parsley
5 cups undrained canned tomatoes
2 cups hot cooked rice
¼ cup dried currants
¾ cup roasted blanched almonds
    Parsley sprigs

1. Remove skin from chicken. Mix flour, ½ teaspoon salt, and pinch white pepper. Coat chicken pieces.
2. Melt lard in a large heavy skillet; add chicken and brown on all sides. Remove pieces from skillet and keep hot.
3. Cook onions, peppers, and garlic in the same skillet, stirring occasionally until onion is lightly browned. Blend 1½ teaspoons salt, ½ teaspoon white pepper, curry powder, and thyme. Mix into skillet along with parsley and tomatoes.
4. Arrange chicken in a shallow roasting pan and pour tomato mixture over it. (If it does not cover chicken, add a small amount of water to the skillet in which mixture was cooked and pour liquid over chicken.) Place a cover on pan or cover tightly with aluminum foil.
5. Cook in a 350°F oven about 45 minutes, or until chicken is tender.
6. Arrange chicken in center of a large heated platter and pile the hot rice around it. Stir currants into sauce remaining in the pan and pour over the rice. Scatter almonds over top. Garnish with parsley.

About 6 servings

Chicken with Fruit

1 tablespoon flour
1 teaspoon seasoned salt
¼ teaspoon paprika
3 pounds broiler-fryer chicken
    pieces (legs, thighs, and breasts)
1½ tablespoons vegetable oil
1½ tablespoons butter or margarine
1 glove garlic, crushed in a garlic
    press or minced
⅓ cup chicken broth
2 tablespoons cider vinegar
1 tablespoon brown sugar
¼ teaspoon rosemary
1 can (11 ounces) mandarin
    oranges, drained; reserve syrup
1 jar (4 ounces) maraschino
    cherries, drained; reserve syrup
1 tablespoon water
1 tablespoon cornstarch
½ cup dark seedless raisins
    Cooked rice

1. Mix flour, seasoned salt, and paprika. Coat chicken pieces.
2. Heat oil, butter, and garlic in a large heavy skillet. Add chicken pieces and brown well on all sides.
3. Mix broth, vinegar, brown sugar, rosemary, and reserved syrups. Pour into skillet; cover and cook slowly 25 minutes, or until chicken is tender.
4. Remove chicken pieces to a serving dish and keep warm; skim any excess fat from liquid in skillet. Blend water with cornstarch and stir into liquid in skillet. Add raisins, bring to boiling, stirring constantly, and cook about 5 minutes, or until mixture is thickened and smooth. Mix in orange sections and cherries; heat thoroughly.
5. Pour sauce over chicken and serve with hot fluffy rice.

About 6 servings

Chicken Livers and Mushrooms

2 pounds chicken livers, thawed if
    frozen
½ cup enriched all-purpose flour
1 teaspoon salt
¼ teaspoon ground white pepper
⅓ cup butter or margarine
1 cup orange sections, cut in halves
1 can (6 ounces) broiled mushrooms
    Fresh parsley, snipped

1. Rinse chicken livers and drain on absorbent paper. Mix flour, salt, and pepper; coat chicken livers evenly.
2. Heat butter in a large skillet, add chicken livers, and cook 10 minutes, or until livers are lightly browned and tender. Mix in orange sections; heat.
3. Meanwhile, heat mushrooms in their broth in a small skillet.
4. Arrange cooked chicken livers and heated orange sections on a hot platter. Top with mushrooms and sprinkle with parsley. Serve immediately.

About 6 servings

Chicken Mexicana

3 tablespoons vegetable oil
2 broiler-fryer chickens (2½ to 3
    pounds each), cut in serving-size
    pieces
2 cans (8 ounces each) tomato sauce
1 can (13¾ ounces) chicken broth
2 tablespoons (½ envelope) dry onion
    soup mix
¾ cup chopped onion
1 clove garlic, minced
6 tablespoons crunchy peanut butter
½ cup cream
½ teaspoon chili powder
¼ cup dry sherry
    Cooked rice

1. Heat oil in a large skillet. Add chicken and brown on all sides.
2. Meanwhile, combine tomato sauce, 1 cup chicken broth, soup mix, onion, and garlic in a saucepan. Heat thoroughly, stirring constantly.
3. Pour sauce over chicken in skillet. Simmer, covered, 20 minutes.
4. Put peanut butter into a bowl and blend in cream and remaining chicken broth; stir into skillet along with chili powder and sherry. Heat thoroughly. Serve with hot fluffy rice.

About 6 servings

Stuffed Roast Capon

½ **cup butter or margarine**
1½ **teaspoons salt**
¼ **teaspoon ground black pepper**
¼ **teaspoon thyme**
¼ **teaspoon marjoram**
¼ **teaspoon rosemary**
1½ **quarts soft enriched bread cubes**
½ **cup milk**
¼ **cup chopped celery leaves**
¼ **cup chopped onion**
1 **capon (6 to 7 pounds)**
 Salt
 Fat, melted

1. For stuffing, melt butter and mix in salt, pepper, thyme, marjoram, and rosemary.
2. Put bread cubes into a large bowl and pour in seasoned butter; lightly toss. Mix in milk, celery leaves, and onion.
3. Rub body and neck cavities of capon with salt. Fill cavities lightly with stuffing; truss bird, using skewers and cord.
4. Place, breast side up, on rack in a shallow roasting pan. Brush skin with melted fat and cover with a fat-moistened cheesecloth.
5. Roast in a 325°F oven 2½ hours, or until a meat thermometer inserted in center of inside thigh muscle registers 180° to 185°F. For easier carving, allow capon to stand about 20 minutes after removing from oven. Serve on a heated platter.

6 to 8 servings

Turkey 'n' Dressing Bake

3 **tablespoons butter or margarine**
½ **cup diced celery**
¼ **cup minced onion**
3¼ **cups chicken broth (dissolve 4 chicken bouillon cubes in 3¼ cups boiling water)**
5 **cups coarse whole wheat bread crumbs; reserve ½ cup crumbs for topping**
¼ **cup snipped parsley**
½ **teaspoon salt**
¼ **teaspoon ground black pepper**
1 **egg, slightly beaten**
2 **tablespoons flour**
2 **eggs, beaten**
⅛ **teaspoon ground black pepper**
¼ **teaspoon crushed leaf sage**
¼ **teaspoon celery salt**
 Thin slices of cooked turkey roast (see Note)
1 **tablespoon butter or margarine, melted**
 Parsley, snipped

1. Heat 3 tablespoons butter in a large skillet. Mix in celery and onion and cook about 5 minutes. Combine vegetables with 1¾ cups chicken broth, 4½ cups bread crumbs, ¼ cup parsley, salt, ¼ teaspoon pepper, and 1 egg. Mix lightly with a fork. Spoon the mixture over bottom of a shallow 2-quart baking dish; set aside.
2. Mix flour and ¼ cup cool broth in a saucepan until smooth; heat until bubbly. Add remaining broth gradually, stirring constantly. Cook and stir over medium heat until sauce comes to boiling; cook 2 minutes. Remove from heat and gradually add to eggs while beating. Blend in remaining pepper, sage, and celery salt.
3. Arrange the desired amount of turkey over dressing in baking dish. Pour the sauce over all.
4. Toss reserved bread crumbs with melted butter; spoon over top.
5. Bake at 350°F 30 to 40 minutes, or until egg mixture is set. Garnish generously with parsley.

6 servings

Note: Prepare frozen boneless turkey roast, following package directions.

Roast Turkey with Herbed Stuffing

Cooked Giblets and Broth
4 quarts ½-inch enriched bread
   cubes
1 cup snipped parsley
2 to 2½ teaspoons salt
2 teaspoons thyme
2 teaspoons rosemary, crushed
2 teaspoons marjoram
1 teaspoon ground sage
1 cup butter or margarine
1 cup coarsely chopped onion
1 cup coarsely chopped celery with
   leaves
1 turkey (14 to 15 pounds)
   Fat
3 tablespoons flour
¼ teaspoon salt
⅛ teaspoon ground black pepper

1. Prepare Cooked Giblets and Broth. Measure 1 cup chopped cooked giblets; set the broth aside.
2. Combine bread cubes, reserved giblets, and parsley in a large bowl. Blend salt, thyme, rosemary, marjoram, and sage; add to bread mixture and toss to mix.
3. Heat butter in a skillet. Mix in onion and celery; cook about 5 minutes, stirring occasionally. Toss with the bread mixture.
4. Add 1 to 2 cups broth (depending upon how moist a stuffing is desired), mixing lightly until ingredients are thoroughly blended.
5. Rinse turkey with cold water; pat dry, inside and out, with absorbent paper. Lightly fill body and neck cavities with the stuffing. Fasten neck skin to back with a skewer. Bring wing tips onto back of bird. Push drumsticks under band of skin at tail, if present, or tie to tail with cord.
6. Place turkey, breast side up, on rack in a shallow roasting pan. Brush skin with fat. Insert meat thermometer in the thickest part of the inner thigh muscle, being sure that tip does not touch bone.
7. Roast in a 325°F oven about 5 hours, or until thermometer registers 180° to 185°F. If desired, baste or brush bird occasionally with pan drippings. Place turkey on a heated platter; for easier carving, allow turkey to stand about 30 minutes.
8. Meanwhile, leaving brown residue in roasting pan, pour remaining drippings and fat into a bowl. Allow fat to rise to surface; skim off fat and measure 3 tablespoons into roasting pan. Blend flour, salt, and pepper with fat. Cook and stir until bubbly. Continue to stir while slowly adding 2 cups reserved liquid (broth and drippings). Cook, stirring constantly, until gravy thickens; scrape pan to blend in brown residue. Cook 1 to 2 minutes. If desired, mix in finely chopped cooked giblets the last few minutes of cooking.

About 25 servings

Cooked Giblets and Broth: Put **turkey neck** and **giblets** (except liver) into a saucepan with **1 large onion,** sliced, **parsley, celery with leaves, 1 medium bay leaf, 2 teaspoons salt,** and **1 quart water.** Cover, bring to boiling, reduce heat, and simmer until giblets are tender (about 2 hours); add the liver the last 15 minutes of cooking. Strain through a colander or sieve; reserve broth for stuffing. Chop giblets; set aside for stuffing and gravy.

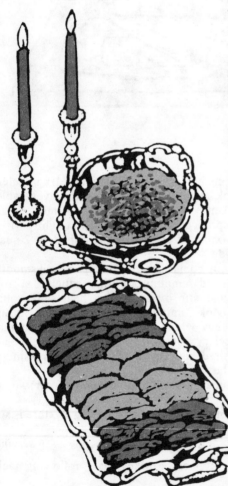

Turkey-Oyster Casserole

1 tablespoon butter
2 teaspoons grated onion
4 ounces mushrooms, sliced
    lengthwise
¼ cup butter
¼ cup enriched all-purpose flour
1 teaspoon salt
¼ teaspoon ground pepper
    Few grains cayenne pepper
2 cups milk
1 egg yolk, slightly beaten
2 tablespoons chopped parsley
¼ teaspoon thyme
2 drops Tabasco
1 pint oysters (with liquor)
2 cups diced cooked turkey
    Buttered soft enriched bread
    crumbs

1. Heat 1 tablespoon butter with onion in a skillet; add mushrooms and cook over medium heat until lightly browned, stirring occasionally. Set aside.
2. Heat ¼ cup butter in a saucepan over low heat. Stir in flour, salt, pepper, and cayenne; cook until bubbly. Add milk gradually, stirring until well blended. Bring rapidly to boiling and boil 1 to 2 minutes, stirring constantly.
3. Blend a small amount of the hot sauce into egg yolk and return to remaining sauce, stirring until mixed. Stir in parsley, thyme, and Tabasco.
4. Heat oysters just to boiling; drain. Add oysters, turkey, and the mushrooms to sauce; toss lightly until thoroughly mixed.
5. Turn mixture into a buttered shallow 1½-quart baking dish. Sprinkle with crumbs.
6. Heat in a 400°F oven about 10 minutes, or until mixture is bubbly around edges and crumbs are golden brown.

About 6 servings

Roast Goose with Rice-and-Pickle Stuffing

3 cups cooked rice; or 1 package (6
    ounces) seasoned white and
    wild rice mix, cooked following
    package directions
1 package (7 ounces) herb-seasoned
    stuffing croutons
2 medium navel oranges, pared and
    sectioned
2 onions, chopped
1 cup cranberries, rinsed, sorted,
    and chopped
1 cup sweet mixed pickles, drained
    and chopped
¼ cup sweet pickle liquid
½ to ¾ cup butter or margarine,
    melted
2 tablespoons brown sugar
1 goose (8 to 10 pounds)
1 tablespoon salt
¼ teaspoon ground black pepper
2 tablespoons light corn syrup
1½ cups orange juice
½ cup orange marmalade

1. Combine rice, stuffing croutons, orange sections, onions, cranberries, pickles and liquid, butter, and brown sugar in a large bowl; toss lightly until blended.
2. Rinse goose and remove any large layers of fat from the body cavity. Pat dry with absorbent paper. Rub body and neck cavities with salt and pepper.
3. Lightly spoon stuffing into the neck and body cavities. Overlap neck cavity with the skin and skewer to back of goose. Close body cavity with skewers and lace with cord. Loop cord around legs; tighten slightly and tie to a skewer inserted in the back above tail. Rub skin of goose with a little salt, if desired.
4. Put remaining stuffing into a greased casserole and cover; or cook in heavy-duty aluminum foil. Set in oven with goose during final hour of roasting.
5. Place goose, breast side down, on a rack in a large shallow roasting pan.
6. Roast in a 325°F oven 2 hours, removing fat from pan several times during this period.
7. Turn goose, breast side up. Blend corn syrup and 1 cup orange juice. Brush generously over goose. Roast about 1½ hours, or until goose tests done. To test for doneness, move leg gently by grasping end of bone; when done, drumstick-thigh joint moves easily or twists out. Brush frequently during final roasting period with the orange-syrup blend.
8. Transfer goose to a heated serving platter. Spoon 2 tablespoons drippings, the remaining ½ cup orange juice, and marmalade into a small saucepan. Heat thoroughly, stirring to blend. Pour into a serving dish or gravy boat to accompany goose.

6 to 8 servings

Rock Cornish Hens with Fruited Stuffing

1½ cups herb-seasoned stuffing
    croutons
½ cup drained canned apricot
    halves, cut in pieces
½ cup quartered seedless green
    grapes
⅓ cup chopped pecans
¼ cup butter or margarine, melted
2 tablespoons apricot nectar
1 tablespoon chopped parsley
¼ teaspoon salt
4 Rock Cornish hens (1 to 1½
    pounds each), thawed if
    purchased frozen
    Salt and pepper
⅓ cup apricot nectar
2 teaspoons soy sauce

1. Combine stuffing croutons, apricots, grapes, pecans, 2 tablespoons butter, 2 tablespoons apricot nectar, parsley, and ¼ teaspoon salt in a bowl; mix lightly.

2. Sprinkle cavities of hens with salt and pepper. Fill each hen with about ½ cup stuffing; fasten with skewers and lace with cord.

3. Blend ⅓ cup apricot nectar, soy sauce, and remaining butter. Place hens, breast side up, on a rack in a shallow roasting pan; brush generously with sauce.

4. Roast in a 350°F oven about 1½ hours, or until hens are tender and well browned; baste occasionally with sauce during roasting.

4 servings

Glazed Duckling Gourmet

2 ducklings (about 4 pounds each),
    quartered (do not use wings,
    necks, and backs) and skinned
1½ teaspoons salt
¼ teaspoon ground nutmeg
3 to 4 tablespoons butter
1 clove garlic, minced
1½ teaspoons rosemary, crushed
1½ teaspoons thyme
1½ cups Burgundy
2 teaspoons red wine vinegar
⅓ cup currant jelly
2 teaspoons cornstarch
2 tablespoons cold water
1½ cups halved seedless green grapes
    Watercress

1. Remove excess fat from duckling pieces; rinse duckling and pat dry with absorbent paper. Rub pieces with salt and nutmeg.

2. Heat butter and garlic in a large skillet over medium heat; add the duckling pieces and brown well on all sides.

3. Add rosemary, thyme, Burgundy, vinegar, and jelly to skillet. Bring to boiling; cover and simmer over low heat until duckling is tender (about 45 minutes). Remove duckling to a heated platter and keep it warm.

4. Combine cornstarch and water; blend into liquid in skillet; bring to boiling and cook 1 to 2 minutes, stirring constantly. Add grapes and toss them lightly until thoroughly heated.

5. Pour the hot sauce over duckling; garnish platter with watercress.

6 to 8 servings

Fish and Shellfish

If you are not a fish lover, you've probably never eaten it properly prepared. Remember, fish is cooked when its flesh becomes opaque and when it flakes easily; overcooking destroys its subtle flavor. Generally high in protein and low in fat, fish is an ideal dish for weight watchers and for those who are trying to control their cholesterol level.

Here are a few pointers to keep in mind when shopping. *Whole fish* are sold just as they were when they came out of the water; *drawn fish* have been eviscerated (entrails removed). *Dressed fish* have been scaled and eviscerated. *Fish steaks* are slices of large fish, cut crosswise through the backbone, and *fillets* are the sides of fish. Fresh fish should have springy flesh, bright eyes, shiny scales, reddish gills, and a mild odor. Frozen fish should be solidly frozen and well wrapped.

Salmon Bake

> 1 **can (16 ounces) salmon, drained and flaked**
> 1½ **cups herb-seasoned stuffing croutons**
> 2 **tablespoons finely snipped parsley**
> 2 **tablespoons finely chopped onion**
> 3 **eggs, well beaten**
> 1 **can (10½ ounces) condensed cream of celery soup**
> ½ **cup milk**
> ⅛ **teaspoon ground black pepper**
> **Lemon, thinly sliced and cut in quarter-slices**
> **Parsley, snipped**
> **Sour cream sauce (prepared from a mix)**

1. Toss salmon, stuffing croutons, parsley, and onion together in a bowl. Blend eggs, condensed soup, milk, and pepper; add to salmon mixture and mix thoroughly. Turn into a greased 1½-quart casserole.
2. Bake at 350°F about 50 minutes. Garnish center with overlapping quarter-slices of lemon and parsley.
3. Serve with hot sour cream sauce.

About 6 servings

Two-Layer Salmon-Rice Loaf

Salmon layer:
- 1 can (16 ounces) salmon
- 2 cups coarse soft enriched bread crumbs
- 2 tablespoons finely chopped onion
- ½ cup undiluted evaporated milk
- 1 egg, slightly beaten
- 2 tablespoons butter or margarine, melted
- 1 tablespoon lemon juice
- 1 teaspoon salt

Rice layer:
- 3 cups cooked enriched rice
- ¼ cup finely chopped parsley
- 2 eggs, slightly beaten
- ⅔ cup undiluted evaporated milk
- 2 tablespoons butter or margarine, melted
- ¼ teaspoon salt

Sauce:
- 1 large onion, quartered and thinly sliced
- ¾ cup water
- 1 can (10¾ ounces) condensed tomato soup

1. For salmon layer, drain salmon and remove skin. Flake salmon and put into a bowl. Add bread crumbs, onion, evaporated milk, egg, butter, lemon juice, and salt; mix lightly. Turn into a buttered 9×5×3-inch loaf pan; press lightly to form a layer.
2. For rice layer, combine rice with parsley, eggs, evaporated milk, butter, and salt. Spoon over salmon layer; press lightly.
3. Set filled loaf pan in a shallow pan. Pour hot water into pan to a depth of 1 inch.
4. Bake at 375°F about 45 minutes. Remove from water immediately.
5. Meanwhile, for sauce, put onion and water into a saucepan. Bring to boiling, reduce heat, and simmer, covered, 10 minutes. Remove onion, if desired. Add condensed soup to saucepan, stir until blended, and bring to boiling.
6. Cut loaf into slices and top servings with tomato sauce.

About 8 servings

Broiled Salmon

- 6 salmon steaks, cut ½ inch thick
- 1 cup sauterne
- ½ cup vegetable oil
- 2 tablespoons wine vinegar
- 2 teaspoons soy sauce
- 2 tablespoons chopped green onion
- Seasoned salt
- Green onion, chopped (optional)
- Pimento strips (optional)

1. Put salmon steaks into a large shallow dish. Mix sauterne, oil, wine vinegar, soy sauce, and green onion; pour over salmon. Marinate in refrigerator several hours or overnight, turning occasionally.
2. To broil, remove steaks from marinade and place on broiler rack. Set under broiler with top 6 inches from heat. Broil about 5 minutes on each side, brushing generously with marinade several times. About 2 minutes before removing from broiler, sprinkle each steak lightly with seasoned salt and, if desired, top with green onion and pimento. Serve at once.

6 servings

Broiled Trout

- Trout (8- to 10-ounce fish for each serving)
- French dressing
- Instant minced onion
- Salt

1. Remove head and fins from trout, if desired. Rinse trout quickly under running cold water; dry thoroughly. Brush inside of fish with French dressing and sprinkle generously with instant minced onion and salt. Brush outside generously with French dressing.

Lemon slices
Tomato wedges
Mint sprigs or watercress

2. Arrange trout in a greased shallow baking pan or on a broiler rack. Place under broiler with top of fish about 3 inches from heat. Broil 5 to 8 minutes on each side, or until fish flakes easily; brush with dressing during broiling.
3. Remove trout to heated serving platter and garnish with lemon, tomato, and mint.

Trout Amandine with Pineapple

6 whole trout
Lemon juice
Enriched all-purpose flour
6 tablespoons butter or margarine
Salt and pepper
2 tablespoons butter or margarine
½ cup slivered blanched almonds
6 well-drained canned pineapple slices
Paprika
Lemon wedges

1. Rinse trout quickly under running cold water; dry thoroughly. Brush trout inside and out with lemon juice. Coat with flour.
2. Heat 6 tablespoons butter in a large skillet. Add trout and brown on both sides. Season with salt and pepper.
3. Meanwhile, heat 2 tablespoons butter in another skillet over low heat. Add almonds and stir occasionally until golden.
4. Sprinkle pineapple slices with paprika. Place pineapple in skillet with almonds and brown lightly on both sides. Arrange trout on a warm serving platter and top with pineapple slices and almonds. Garnish platter with lemon wedges.

6 servings

Planked Halibut Dinner

4 halibut steaks, fresh or thawed frozen (about 2 pounds)
¼ cup butter, melted
2 tablespoons olive oil
1 tablespoon wine vinegar
2 teaspoons lemon juice
1 clove garlic, minced
¼ teaspoon dry mustard
¼ teaspoon marjoram
⅛ teaspoon salt
⅛ teaspoon ground black pepper
2 large zucchini
1 package (10 ounces) frozen green peas
1 can (8¼ ounces) tiny whole carrots
Au Gratin Potato Puffs
Butter
Fresh parsley
Lemon wedges

1. Place halibut steaks in an oiled baking pan.
2. Combine butter, olive oil, vinegar, lemon juice, garlic, dry mustard, marjoram, salt, and pepper. Drizzle over halibut.
3. Bake at 450°F 10 to 12 minutes, or until halibut is almost done.
4. Meanwhile, halve zucchini lengthwise and scoop out center portion. Cook in boiling salted water until just tender.
5. Cook peas following directions on package. Heat carrots.
6. Prepare Au Gratin Potato Puffs.
7. Arrange halibut on wooden plank or heated ovenware platter and border with zucchini halves filled with peas, carrots, and potato puffs. Dot peas and carrots with butter.
8. Place platter under broiler to brown potato puffs. Sprinkle carrots with chopped parsley.
9. Garnish with sprigs of parsley and lemon wedges arranged on a skewer.

4 servings

Au Gratin Potato Puffs: Pare 1½ pounds potatoes; cook and mash potatoes in a saucepan. Add **2 tablespoons butter** and ⅓ cup milk; whip until fluffy. Add **2 slightly beaten egg yolks,** ½ cup shredded sharp Cheddar cheese, 1 teaspoon salt, and few grains pepper; continue whipping. Using a pastry bag with a large star tip, form mounds about 2 inches in diameter on plank. Proceed as directed in recipe.

Baked Fish with Shrimp Stuffing

1 dressed whitefish, bass, or lake
    trout (2 to 3 pounds)
  Salt
1 cup chopped cooked shrimp
1 cup chopped fresh mushrooms
1 cup soft enriched bread crumbs
½ cup chopped celery
¼ cup chopped onion
2 tablespoons chopped parsley
¾ teaspoon salt
  Few grains black pepper
½ teaspoon thyme
¼ cup butter or margarine, melted
2 to 3 tablespoons apple cider
2 tablespoons butter or margarine,
    melted
  Parsley sprigs

1. Rinse fish under running cold water; drain well and pat dry with absorbent paper. Sprinkle fish cavity generously with salt.
2. Combine in a bowl the shrimp, mushrooms, bread crumbs, celery, onion, parsley, salt, pepper, and thyme. Pour ¼ cup melted butter gradually over bread mixture, tossing lightly until mixed.
3. Pile stuffing lightly into fish. Fasten with skewers and lace with cord. Place fish in a greased large shallow baking pan. Mix cider and 2 tablespoons melted butter; brush over fish.
4. Bake at 375°F, brushing occasionally with cider mixture, 25 to 30 minutes, or until fish flakes easily when pierced with a fork. If additional browning is desired, place fish under broiler 3 to 5 minutes. Transfer to a heated platter and remove skewers and cord. Garnish platter with parsley.

4 to 6 servings

California Style Red Snapper Steaks

6 fresh or thawed frozen red snapper
    steaks (about 2 pounds)
  Salt and pepper
¼ cup butter or margarine, melted
1 tablespoon grated orange peel
¼ cup orange juice
1 teaspoon lemon juice
  Dash nutmeg
  Fresh orange sections

1. Arrange red snapper steaks in a single layer in a well-greased baking pan; season with salt and pepper.
2. Combine butter, orange peel and juice, lemon juice, and nutmeg; pour over fish.
3. Bake at 350°F 20 to 25 minutes, or until fish flakes easily when tested with a fork.
4. To serve, put steaks onto a warm platter; spoon sauce in pan over them. Garnish with orange sections.

6 servings

Sole with Tangerine Sauce

1 pound sole fillets
5 tablespoons butter or margarine
2 teaspoons finely shredded tangerine
    peel
½ cup tangerine juice
1 teaspoon lemon juice
1 tablespoon finely chopped parsley
1 tablespoon finely chopped green
    onion
1 bay leaf
1 tangerine, peeled, sectioned, and
    seeds removed
3 tablespoons flour
½ teaspoon salt
⅛ teaspoon ground black pepper
3 tablespoons butter or margarine
  Parsley

1. Thaw fish if frozen.
2. Combine 5 tablespoons butter, tangerine peel and juice, lemon juice, 1 tablespoon parsley, green onion, and bay leaf in a saucepan. Bring to boiling and simmer over low heat until slightly thickened, stirring occasionally. Remove from heat; remove bay leaf and mix in tangerine sections. Keep sauce hot.
3. Mix flour, salt, and pepper; coat fish fillets. Heat 3 tablespoons butter in a skillet. Add fillets and fry until both sides are browned and fish flakes easily when tested with a fork.
4. Arrange fish on a hot platter and pour the hot sauce over it. Garnish with parsley.

About 4 servings

Tuna Fiesta

1 can (6½ or 7 ounces) tuna, drained and separated in large pieces
1 can (16 ounces) stewed tomatoes, drained
1 can (15¼ ounces) spaghetti in tomato sauce with cheese
1 tablespoon ketchup
1 teaspoon seasoned salt
½ cup (about 2 ounces) shredded sharp Cheddar cheese
   Few grains paprika
   Fresh parsley

1. Turn tuna, stewed tomatoes, and spaghetti into a saucepan. Add ketchup, seasoned salt, cheese, and paprika; mix well. Set over medium heat, stirring occasionally, until thoroughly heated (about 8 minutes).
2. Turn into a warm serving dish; garnish with parsley. Serve at once.

About 6 servings

Note: If desired, reserve cheese and paprika for topping. Mix remaining ingredients and turn into a greased 1-quart casserole. Top with the cheese and paprika. Set in a 350°F oven 20 minutes, or until thoroughly heated. Garnish with parsley.

Patio Crab Casserole

¼ cup butter or margarine
2 cups chopped onion
1 pound frozen or 2 cans (7½ ounces each) Alaska king crab, drained and sliced
½ cup snipped parsley
2 tablespoons capers
2 tablespoons snipped chives
2 pimentos, diced
1½ cups corn muffin mix
⅛ teaspoon salt
1 egg, fork beaten
½ cup milk
1 cup cream-style golden corn
6 drops Tabasco
2 cups dairy sour cream
1½ cups shredded extra sharp Cheddar cheese

1. Heat butter in a skillet. Add onion and cook until tender. Stir in crab, parsley, capers, chives, and pimentos; heat.
2. Meanwhile, stir corn muffin mix, salt, egg, milk, corn, and Tabasco until just moistened (batter should be lumpy). Turn into a greased shallow 3-quart dish and spread evenly to edges.
3. Spoon crab mixture and then sour cream over batter. Sprinkle cheese over all.
4. Bake at 400°F 25 to 30 minutes.
5. To serve, cut into squares.

About 12 servings

Savory Oysters

⅓ cup butter or margarine
1 can (4 ounces) sliced mushrooms, drained
⅓ cup chopped green pepper
½ clove garlic
2 cups coarse toasted enriched bread crumbs
1 quart oysters, drained (reserve liquor)
¼ cup cream
1 teaspoon Worcestershire sauce
1 teaspoon salt
1 teaspoon paprika
⅛ teaspoon ground mace
   Few grains cayenne pepper

1. Heat butter in a large skillet. Add mushrooms, green pepper, and garlic; cook about 5 minutes. Remove skillet from heat; discard garlic. Stir in toasted bread crumbs. Set aside.
2. Mix ¼ cup reserved oyster liquor, cream, and Worcestershire sauce.
3. Blend salt, paprika, mace, and cayenne.
4. Use about a third of crumb mixture to form a layer in bottom of a greased 2-quart casserole. Arrange about half of oysters and half of seasonings over crumbs. Repeat crumb layer, then oyster and seasoning layers. Pour the liquid mixture over all. Top with remaining crumbs.
5. Bake at 375°F 20 to 30 minutes, or until thoroughly heated and crumbs are golden brown.

6 to 8 servings

Scallops Gourmet

2 pounds scallops
1 cup boiling water
1 teaspoon salt
3 to 4 tablespoons lemon juice
1 medium onion, sliced
2 sprigs parsley
1 bay leaf
¼ cup butter or margarine
½ pound mushrooms, sliced
   lengthwise
3 tomatoes, peeled and diced
2 tablespoons butter or margarine
2 tablespoons flour
¼ teaspoon garlic powder
8 patty shells, heated
   Carrot curls

1. Rinse scallops under running cold water. Put scallops into a saucepan and pour boiling water over them. Stir in salt, lemon juice, onion, parsley, and bay leaf. Cook, covered, over low heat 5 minutes; drain and reserve 1 cup of the stock. If scallops are large, cut into smaller pieces. Set aside.
2. Heat ¼ cup butter in a skillet. Add mushrooms and cook until delicately browned and tender, stirring occasionally. Remove from skillet with slotted spoon; set aside. Add diced tomatoes to skillet and cook 5 minutes. Set aside.
3. Heat 2 tablespoons butter in a saucepan. Blend in flour; heat until bubbly. Add reserved stock gradually, stirring constantly. Continue to stir and bring rapidly to boiling; cook 1 to 2 minutes.
4. Add scallops, mushrooms, tomatoes, and garlic powder to sauce; heat thoroughly.
5. To serve, spoon scallop mixture into patty shells. Garnish with carrot curls.

About 8 servings

Seafood Kabobs

1 lobster tail (8 ounces), cut in 6
   pieces
6 scallops
6 shrimp, peeled and deveined
12 large mushroom caps
½ cup olive oil
3 tablespoons soy sauce
1 tablespoon Worcestershire sauce
2 tablespoons white wine vinegar
½ teaspoon grated lemon peel
2 tablespoons lemon juice
½ teaspoon ground pepper
2 teaspoons snipped parsley
18 (4-inch) pieces sliced bacon
12 (1-inch) squares green pepper
6 cherry tomatoes

1. Put lobster pieces, scallops, shrimp, and mushroom caps into a shallow dish.
2. Combine olive oil, soy sauce, Worcestershire sauce, vinegar, lemon peel. lemon juice, pepper, and parsley in a screwtop jar and shake vigorously. Pour the marinade over the seafood and mushroom caps and set aside for at least 2 hours.
3. Drain off marinade and reserve.
4. Wrap each piece of seafood in bacon. Thread pieces on skewers (about 10 inches each) as follows: green pepper, lobster, mushroom, scallop, mushroom, shrimp, and green pepper. Arrange on a broiler rack and brush with marinade.
5. Place under broiler 3 inches from heat. Broil 10 to 12 minutes, turning and brushing frequently with marinade. Add a cherry tomato to each skewer during the last few minutes of broiling.

6 servings

Deviled Crab

Mustard Sauce:
- 2 tablespoons dry mustard
- 2 tablespoons water
- 2 tablespoons olive oil
- 1 tablespoon ketchup
- ¼ teaspoon salt
- ¼ teaspoon Worcestershire sauce

Crab meat mixture:
- 6 tablespoons butter
- 4 teaspoons finely chopped green pepper
- 2 teaspoons finely chopped onion
- 6 tablespoons flour
- 1 teaspoon salt
- ½ teaspoon dry mustard
- 1½ cups milk
- 1 teaspoon Worcestershire sauce
- 2 egg yolks, slightly beaten
- 1 pound lump crab meat, drained
- 2 teaspoons chopped pimento
- 2 tablespoons dry sherry
- 1 cup fine dry enriched bread crumbs
- Paprika
- Butter, melted

1. For Mustard Sauce, blend dry mustard, water, olive oil, ketchup, salt, and Worcestershire sauce in a small bowl; set aside.

2. For crab meat mixture, heat butter in a large heavy saucepan. Add green pepper and onion; cook until onion is golden in color.

3. Blend flour, salt, and dry mustard; stir in. Heat until bubbly. Add milk gradually, stirring until smooth. Stir in Worcestershire sauce. Bring rapidly to boiling; cook 1 to 2 minutes.

4. Remove mixture from heat and stir a small amount of hot mixture into the egg yolks; return to saucepan and cook 3 to 5 minutes, stirring constantly.

5. Stir in crab meat and pimento; heat thoroughly. Remove from heat and blend in sherry and the Mustard Sauce.

6. Spoon into 6 shell-shaped ramekins, allowing about ½ cup mixture for each. Sprinkle top with bread crumbs and paprika; drizzle with melted butter.

7. Set in a 450°F oven about 6 minutes, or until tops are lightly browned and mixture is thoroughly heated. Serve hot.

6 servings

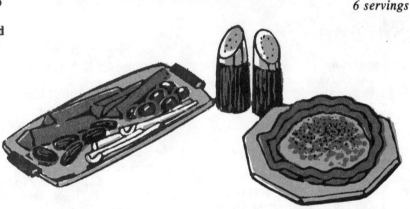

Baked Flounder Superb

- 2 pounds flounder fillets
- ½ cup fine Melba toast crumbs
- ¼ cup butter or margarine, melted
- ⅔ cup minced green onion
- 2 tablespoons snipped parsley
- ½ teaspoon poultry seasoning
- ½ pound fresh or thawed frozen sea scallops, chopped
- 1 can (4 ounces) mushroom stems and pieces, drained
- 2 tablespoons butter or margarine
- 2 tablespoons flour
- ¼ teaspoon salt
- Few grains black pepper
- 1 cup milk
- Shredded Parmesan cheese

1. Thaw fish if frozen; cut fish into 12 pieces.

2. Toss crumbs and melted butter together in a bowl. Add green onion, parsley, poultry seasoning, scallops, and mushrooms; mix well.

3. Place a piece of flounder in the bottom of each of 6 ramekins. Spoon stuffing mixture over flounder and top with remaining flounder pieces.

4. Heat butter in a saucepan. Stir in flour, salt, and pepper and cook until bubbly. Add milk gradually, stirring until smooth. Bring rapidly to boiling; boil 1 to 2 minutes, stirring constantly.

5. Spoon sauce over flounder. Sprinkle with Parmesan cheese.

6. Bake at 350°F 20 to 25 minutes. If desired, set ramekins under broiler with tops about 3 inches from heat until lightly browned; watch carefully to avoid overbrowning.

6 servings

Shrimp Exotica

1½ pounds deveined cooked shrimp
1 can (20 ounces) sliced pineapple, drained; reserve syrup
2 cups water
3 chicken bouillon cubes
1 cup long-grain enriched white rice
¼ cup vegetable oil
1½ cups cubed cooked ham
¼ cup chopped onion
1 clove garlic, crushed in a garlic press or minced
2 tablespoons chopped preserved or crystallized ginger
2 teaspoons soy sauce
2 teaspoons curry powder
½ teaspoon salt
1 medium green pepper, cut in strips

1. Reserve 5 or 6 whole shrimp for garnish. Cut remaining shrimp into pieces. Set aside. Cut 4 pineapple slices into pieces and set aside.
2. Bring water to boiling in a deep saucepan. Add the bouillon cubes, and when dissolved, add the rice gradually, so boiling continues. Cover pan tightly, reduce heat, and simmer 15 to 20 minutes, until a kernel is soft when pressed between fingers.
3. Heat oil in a large skillet. Add ham, onion, and garlic; heat thoroughly, turning with a spoon.
4. Blend ⅔ cup of the reserved pineapple syrup with ginger, soy sauce, curry powder, and salt; add to skillet along with green pepper and heat thoroughly. Add rice and shrimp and remaining pineapple pieces; toss until mixed. Heat thoroughly. Serve on a warm serving platter. Garnish with the pineapple slices and whole shrimp.

About 6 servings

Shrimp Creole

Cooked shrimp:
1 pound fresh shrimp with shells
2 cups water
2 tablespoons lemon juice
2 teaspoons salt

Sauce:
¼ cup fat
¾ cup finely chopped onion
¾ cup minced green pepper
1 can (16 ounces) tomatoes, sieved
1 teaspoon Worcestershire sauce
1 bay leaf
1½ teaspoons salt
¼ teaspoon ground black pepper
½ teaspoon sugar
½ teaspoon oregano
Cooked rice

1. For cooked shrimp, rinse shrimp under running cold water.
2. Combine water, lemon juice, and salt in a saucepan and bring to boiling. Drop shrimp into boiling water, reduce heat, and simmer, covered, until pink and tender (about 5 minutes).
3. Drain shrimp immediately and cover with cold water to chill; drain again. Remove tiny legs and peel shells from shrimp. Cut a slit to just below surface along back (curved surface) of shrimp to expose the black vein. With knife point, remove vein. Rinse shrimp quickly in cold water.
4. Reserve about ten whole shrimp for garnish and cut remainder into pieces. Refrigerate until ready to use.
5. For sauce, heat fat in a large heavy skillet. Mix in onion and green pepper and cook until vegetables are tender. Stir in sieved tomatoes, Worcestershire sauce, bay leaf, salt, pepper, sugar, and oregano. Bring mixture to boiling and simmer, uncovered, stirring occasionally. Cook about 15 minutes, or until thickened. Stir in shrimp pieces and heat thoroughly.
6. Serve shrimp mixture on hot fluffy rice and garnish with the whole shrimp.

About 4 servings

Cereals, Grains, and Pasta

If serving a bowl of rice or spaghetti and meat sauce is the only use you make of the wide variety of grain and pasta products on the market today, read on.

Pasta, rice, and other grains are inexpensive (their value as budget-stretchers is well known) and nutritious. They supply protein, B vitamins, calcium, and iron. Remember to buy enriched pasta and rice—it does make a difference. When pasta or rice is mixed with even small amounts of high-protein foods such as meat or cheese, the nutritional value of the dish increases considerably. Each of the following delicious pasta and grain recipes will let you stay well within your budget and add variety and nutrition to your meals.

Lemony Meat Sauce with Spaghetti

2 pounds ground beef
1½ cups finely chopped onion
1¼ cups chopped green pepper
2 cloves garlic, minced
¼ cup firmly packed brown sugar
1 teaspoon salt
¼ teaspoon ground black pepper
1 teaspoon thyme, crushed
½ teaspoon basil, crushed
2 cups water
2 cans (8 ounces each) tomato sauce
2 cans (6 ounces each) tomato paste
1 can (6 ounces) sliced broiled
 mushrooms (undrained)
1 tablespoon grated lemon peel
¼ cup lemon juice
1 pound enriched spaghetti
 Shredded Parmesan cheese

1. Put meat, onion, green pepper, and garlic into a heated large heavy saucepot or Dutch oven. Cook 10 to 15 minutes, cutting meat apart with fork or spoon.
2. Stir in brown sugar, salt, pepper, thyme, basil, water, tomato sauce, and tomato paste. Cover and simmer 2 to 3 hours, stirring occasionally. About 30 minutes before serving, mix in mushrooms with liquid and lemon peel and juice.
3. Meanwhile, cook spaghetti following package directions; drain.
4. Spoon sauce over hot spaghetti and sprinkle generously with cheese.

10 to 12 servings

Spaghetti à la King Crab

Parmesan Croutons
2 cans (7½ ounces each) Alaska king
  crab or 1 pound frozen Alaska
  king crab
2 tablespoons olive oil
½ cup butter or margarine
4 cloves garlic, minced
1 bunch green onions, sliced
2 medium tomatoes, peeled and diced
½ cup chopped parsley
2 tablespoons lemon juice
¼ teaspoon basil
¼ teaspoon thyme
½ teaspoon salt
1 pound enriched spaghetti

1. Prepare Parmesan Croutons; set aside.
2. Drain canned crab and slice. Or, defrost, drain, and slice frozen crab.
3. Heat olive oil, butter, and garlic in a saucepan. Add crab, green onions, tomatoes, parsley, lemon juice, basil, thyme, and salt. Heat gently 8 to 10 minutes.
4. Meanwhile, cook spaghetti following package directions; drain.
5. Toss spaghetti with king crab sauce. Top with Parmesan Croutons. Pass additional grated Parmesan cheese.

About 6 servings

Parmesan Croutons: Put **3 tablespoons butter** into a shallow baking pan. Set in a 350°F oven until butter is melted. Slice **French bread** into small cubes to make about 1 cup. Toss with melted butter. Return to oven until golden (about 6 minutes). Sprinkle with **2 tablespoons grated Parmesan cheese** and toss.

White Clam Sauce for Linguine

12 ounces enriched linguine
¼ cup olive oil
½ cup chopped onion
¼ cup snipped parsley
3 cloves garlic, minced
2 tablespoons flour
¼ to ½ teaspoon salt
  Few grains pepper
3 cans (8 ounces each) minced
  clams, drained; reserve 1½ cups
  liquid

1. Cook linguine following package directions; drain and keep hot.
2. Meanwhile, heat oil in a large skillet. Add onion, parsley, and garlic; cook about 3 minutes, stirring occasionally.
3. Mix in flour, salt, and pepper; cook until bubbly. Add reserved clam liquid gradually, while blending thoroughly. Bring rapidly to boiling, stirring constantly, and boil 1 to 2 minutes. Mix in the minced clams and heat; do not boil.
4. Serve clam sauce on the hot linguine.

6 servings

Fiesta Zucchini-Tomato Casserole

1½ quarts water
2 packets dry onion soup mix
4 ounces enriched spaghetti, broken
⅓ cup butter or margarine
⅔ cup coarsely chopped onion
1 cup green pepper strips
2 or 3 zucchini (about ¾ pound),
  washed, ends trimmed, and
  zucchini cut in about ½-inch
  slices

1. Bring water to boiling in a saucepot. Add onion soup mix and spaghetti to the boiling water. Partially cover and boil gently about 10 minutes, or until spaghetti is tender. Drain and set spaghetti mixture aside; reserve liquid.*
2. Heat butter in a large heavy skillet. Add onion and green pepper and cook about 3 minutes, or until tender. Add zucchini; cover and cook 5 minutes. Stir in tomatoes, parsley, seasoned salt, and pepper. Cover and cook about 2 minutes, or just until heated.
3. Turn contents of skillet into a 2-quart casserole. Add

4 medium tomatoes, peeled and cut
   in wedges
¼ cup snipped parsley
1 teaspoon seasoned salt
⅛ teaspoon ground black pepper
⅔ cup shredded Swiss cheese

drained spaghetti and toss gently to mix. Sprinkle cheese over top. If necessary to reheat mixture, set in a 350°F oven until thoroughly heated before placing under broiler.
4. Set under broiler with top about 5 inches from heat until cheese is melted and lightly browned.

6 to 8 servings

*The strained soup may be stored for future use as broth or for cooking vegetables, preparing gravy or sauce, or as desired.

Rice Pilaf Deluxe

⅓ cup butter
1½ cups uncooked enriched white rice
⅓ cup chopped onion
1½ teaspoons salt
3 cans (13¾ ounces each) chicken
   broth
¾ cup golden raisins
3 tablespoons butter
¾ cup coarsely chopped pecans
½ teaspoon salt

1. Heat ⅓ cup butter in a heavy skillet. Add rice and onion and cook until lightly browned, stirring frequently.
2. Add 1½ teaspoons salt, chicken broth, and raisins; cover, bring to boiling, reduce heat, and simmer until rice is tender and liquid is absorbed (20 to 25 minutes).
3. Just before serving, heat 3 tablespoons butter in a small skillet. Add pecans and ½ teaspoon salt; heat 2 to 3 minutes, stirring occasionally.
4. Serve rice topped with salted pecans.

About 8 servings

Spanish Rice au Gratin

½ cup uncooked enriched white rice
1 cup water
½ teaspoon salt
1½ tablespoons butter or margarine
½ cup chopped onion
½ cup chopped celery
⅓ cup chopped green pepper
1 cup canned tomatoes, cut in
   pieces
½ teaspoon salt
½ teaspoon monosodium glutamate
1 teaspoon sugar
¾ teaspoon chili powder
¼ teaspoon Worcestershire sauce
1 cup (about 4 ounces) shredded
   Cheddar cheese

1. Combine rice, water, and ½ teaspoon salt in a saucepan. Bring to boiling, reduce heat, and simmer, covered, about 14 minutes.
2. Meanwhile, heat butter in a skillet. Mix in onion, celery, and green pepper. Cook until vegetables are tender. Mix in cooked rice, tomatoes, ½ teaspoon salt, monosodium glutamate, sugar, chili powder, and Worcestershire sauce. Simmer until thick.
3. Turn mixture into a greased baking dish. Top evenly with cheese.
4. Place under broiler 3 to 4 inches from heat until cheese is melted.

3 or 4 servings

Polenta

2 tablespoons olive oil
1 clove garlic, crushed
1 can (8 ounces) sliced mushrooms, drained, or 1 pound fresh mushrooms, sliced
1 can (16 ounces) tomatoes (undrained)
⅓ cup tomato paste
1 teaspoon salt
¼ teaspoon ground pepper
3 cups water
1½ teaspoons salt
1 cup enriched cornmeal
1 cup cold water
Grated Parmesan or Romano cheese

1. Heat olive oil and garlic in a skillet. Add mushrooms and cook about 5 minutes, stirring occasionally. When lightly browned, stir in tomatoes with liquid, tomato paste, salt, and pepper. Simmer 15 to 20 minutes.
2. Meanwhile, bring 3 cups water and 1½ teaspoons salt to boiling in a saucepan. Mix cornmeal and 1 cup cold water; stir into boiling water. Continue boiling, stirring constantly to prevent sticking, until mixture is thick. Cover, reduce heat, and cook over low heat 10 minutes or longer.
3. Turn cooked cornmeal onto warm serving platter and top with the tomato-mushroom mixture. Sprinkle with grated cheese. Serve at once.

6 to 8 servings

Fried Cornmeal Mush

1 cup enriched yellow cornmeal
1 teaspoon salt
2¼ cups milk
1½ cups water
Butter or margarine
Syrup or honey

1. Combine cornmeal, salt, and 1 cup milk. Pour remaining milk and water into a saucepan and bring to boiling. Add cornmeal mixture gradually; cook and stir until thickened. Cover and cook over low heat 10 minutes. Pour into a buttered loaf pan, mold, or other container, and chill.
2. Turn out of pan and slice ½ inch thick. Cook on lightly buttered griddle or skillet until crisp and golden, turning once. Serve with butter and syrup or honey.

6 to 8 servings

Bulgur, Pilaf Style

½ cup butter or margarine
½ cup chopped onion
½ cup chopped green pepper
2 cups bulgur (cracked wheat)
4 cups boiling water
4 chicken bouillon cubes
1 teaspoon salt
¼ teaspoon ground black pepper
1 cup shredded carrot

1. Heat butter in a skillet with heat-resistant handle. Mix in onion and green pepper. Cook until onion is tender.
2. Stir in bulgur, cover, reduce heat, and cook 10 minutes over low heat; stir once or twice to prevent sticking.
3. Add boiling water and bouillon cubes; stir until cubes are dissolved; cover tightly.
4. Cook in a 350°F oven 30 minutes. Stir in salt, pepper, and carrot. Continue cooking 15 minutes, or until liquid is absorbed and bulgur is tender.

About 8 servings

Baked Hominy Grits

1 quart milk
½ cup butter or margarine, cut in pieces
1 cup enriched white hominy grits, quick or long-cooking
1 teaspoon salt

1. Heat milk to boiling. Add butter; then add hominy grits gradually, stirring constantly. Bring to boiling and boil 3 minutes, or until mixture becomes thick, stirring constantly. Remove from heat; add salt.
2. Beat mixture at high speed of an electric mixer 5 minutes, or until grits have a creamy appearance. Turn mixture into a greased 1½-quart casserole.
3. Bake at 350°F about 1 hour. Serve hot.

6 to 8 servings

Vegetables

Have you ever planned a meal around a vegetable? Try it sometime. Each vegetable has its own unique character. Steam your favorite vegetables, or simmer them in a minimum amount of water, and cook just till tender to preserve their texture, color, and nutrients. Then it takes only minutes to give special treatment to simple vegetable dishes.

Of course, vegetables can also be the basis of delicious casseroles and main dishes. Vegetables provide essential vitamins and minerals and the roughage necessary for good digestion. Yellow vegetables, such as squash and carrots, are good providers of vitamin A. Green leafy vegetables supply vitamins A and C and calcium. Potatoes and tomatoes are also important sources of vitamin C. And dried beans and peas contain protein.

Flavor-Rich Baked Beans

1½ quarts water
 1 pound dried navy beans, rinsed
 ½ pound salt pork
 ½ cup chopped celery
 ½ cup chopped onion
 1 teaspoon salt
 ¼ cup ketchup
 ¼ cup molasses
 2 tablespoons brown sugar
 1 teaspoon dry mustard
 ½ teaspoon ground black pepper
 ¼ teaspoon ground ginger

1. Grease 8 individual casseroles having tight-fitting covers. (A 2-quart casserole with lid may be used.)
2. Heat water to boiling in a large heavy saucepan. Add beans gradually to water so that boiling continues. Boil 2 minutes. Remove from heat and set aside 1 hour.
3. Remove rind from salt pork and cut into 1-inch chunks; set aside.
4. Add pork chunks to beans with celery, onion, and salt; mix well. Cover tightly and bring mixture to boiling over high heat. Reduce and simmer 45 minutes, stirring once or twice. Drain beans, reserving liquid.
5. Put an equal amount of beans and salt pork chunks into each casserole.
6. Mix one cup of bean liquid, ketchup, molasses, brown sugar, dry mustard, pepper, and ginger in a saucepan. Bring to boiling. Pour an equal amount of sauce over beans in each casserole. Cover casseroles.
7. Bake at 300°F about 2½ hours. If necessary, add more reserved bean liquid to beans during baking. Remove covers and bake ½ hour longer.

8 servings

Artichokes with Creamy Dill Sauce

Cooked Artichokes
1 cup creamed cottage cheese
½ cup plain yogurt
1 tablespoon lemon juice
1 teaspoon instant minced onion
1 teaspoon sugar
½ teaspoon dill weed
½ teaspoon salt
  Few grains pepper
2 parsley sprigs

1. Prepare desired number of artichokes.
2. Meanwhile, combine cottage cheese, yogurt, lemon juice, onion, sugar, dill weed, salt, pepper, and parsley in an electric blender container. Blend until smooth. Chill.
3. Serve artichokes with sauce for dipping.

About 1½ cups sauce

Cooked Artichokes: Wash **artichokes.** Cut off about 1 inch from tops and bases. Remove and discard lower outside leaves. If desired, snip off tips of remaining leaves. Stand artichokes upright in a deep saucepan large enough to hold them snugly. Add **boiling water** to a depth of 1 inch. Add **salt** (¼ teaspoon for each artichoke). Cover and boil gently 30 to 45 minutes, or until stems can easily be pierced with a fork. Drain artichokes; cut off stems.

Stir-Fry Vegetables and Rice

1 cup brown rice
¼ cup vegetable oil
1 medium onion, thinly sliced
1 cup thinly sliced carrot
1 clove garlic, crushed
1 green pepper, coarsely chopped
1 cup thinly sliced zucchini
1 cup thinly sliced mushrooms
2 cans (16 ounces each) bean sprouts, drained
¼ to ⅓ cup soy sauce

1. Cook rice following package directions; set aside.
2. Heat oil in a large skillet. Add onion, carrot, and garlic; cook and stir over medium high heat about 2 minutes.
3. Add green pepper, zucchini, and mushrooms; cook and stir 2 to 3 minutes.
4. Stir in cooked rice, bean sprouts, and soy sauce. Cook and stir 1 to 2 minutes, or until thoroughly heated.

6 to 8 servings

Tangy Green Beans

¾ pound fresh green beans, cut crosswise in pieces, or 1 package (9 ounces) frozen cut green beans
½ teaspoon salt
¼ cup butter or margarine
1 medium onion, quartered and thinly sliced
1 tablespoon wine vinegar
¼ teaspoon salt
⅛ teaspoon ground black pepper
¼ teaspoon dill weed
⅛ teaspoon crushed savory

1. Put beans and ½ teaspoon salt into a small amount of boiling water in a saucepan. Bring to boiling and cook, covered, until crisp-tender. Drain and set aside.
2. Heat 3 tablespoons butter in a skillet; add onion and cook 3 to 5 minutes. Mix in beans and cook about 4 minutes, or until thoroughly heated, stirring occasionally. Add remaining butter, wine vinegar, ¼ teaspoon salt, pepper, dill, and savory; toss over low heat until butter is melted.

About 4 servings

Planked Halibut Dinner, 53

Butter-Sauced Asparagus

2 pounds fresh asparagus, washed,
    or 2 packages (10 ounces each)
    frozen asparagus spears, cooked
¼ cup butter
¼ cup chopped pecans
¼ cup finely chopped celery
1 tablespoon lemon juice

1. Put fresh asparagus into a small amount of boiling salted water in a skillet, bring to boiling, reduce heat, and cook 5 minutes, uncovered; cover and cook 10 minutes, or until just tender.

2. Meanwhile, heat butter in a small saucepan. Add pecans and celery and cook 5 minutes. Stir in lemon juice. Pour over asparagus and serve immediately.

About 6 servings

Lima Beans New Orleans

1 package (10 ounces) frozen lima
    beans
1 tablespoon vinegar
2 tablespoons olive oil
½ teaspoon salt
    Dash pepper
2 tablespoons chopped parsley
½ clove garlic, minced
1 teaspoon lemon juice

1. Cook lima beans following package directions; drain if necessary.

2. Add vinegar, olive oil, salt, pepper, parsley, and garlic to limas in saucepan. Heat thoroughly, then mix in lemon juice. Serve immediately.

4 servings

Broccoli with Buttery Lemon Crunch

1½ pounds broccoli, washed
¼ cup butter or margarine
½ cup coarse dry enriched bread
    crumbs
1 tablespoon grated lemon peel
3 tablespoons butter or margarine
1 small clove garlic, crushed in a
    garlic press or minced
½ teaspoon salt
    Few grains black pepper

1. Cook broccoli in a small amount of boiling salted water until just tender. (Cook uncovered 5 minutes, then cover and cook 10 to 15 minutes, or cook, covered, the full time and lift the lid 3 or 4 times during cooking.)

2. Meanwhile, heat ¼ cup butter in a large skillet; add bread crumbs and heat, stirring frequently, until well browned. Remove crumbs from butter with a slotted spoon and mix with the lemon peel.

3. Put 3 tablespoons butter, garlic, salt, and pepper into skillet; heat until butter is lightly browned. Add broccoli and turn gently until well coated with butter.

4. Arrange broccoli in a heated vegetable dish and pour remaining garlic butter over it. Top with the "lemoned" crumbs.

About 6 servings

Brussels Sprouts in Herb Butter

2 pounds fresh Brussels sprouts
⅓ cup butter
1 tablespoon grated onion
1 tablespoon lemon juice
¾ teaspoon salt
¼ teaspoon thyme
¼ teaspoon marjoram
¼ teaspoon savory

1. Cook Brussels sprouts in boiling salted water until just tender.

2. Put butter, onion, lemon juice, salt, thyme, marjoram, and savory into a saucepan. Set over low heat until butter is melted, stirring to blend.

3. When Brussels sprouts are tender, drain thoroughly and turn into a warm serving dish. Pour the seasoned butter mixture over the Brussels sprouts and toss gently to coat sprouts evenly and thoroughly.

About 8 servings

Zesty Beets

1 can or jar (16 ounces) small whole
  beets
2 tablespoons butter or margarine
2 tablespoons prepared horseradish
½ teaspoon prepared mustard
½ teaspoon seasoned salt

Heat beets in liquid; drain. Add butter, horseradish, prepared mustard, and seasoned salt; stir gently.

About 4 servings

Cabbage Rolls Paprikash

8 large cabbage leaves
2½ cups diced cooked chicken
2 tablespoons chopped onion
½ cup finely chopped celery
¼ pound chopped fresh mushrooms
1 small clove garlic, minced
½ teaspoon salt
½ teaspoon thyme leaves
1 egg, beaten
2 tablespoons butter or margarine
6 tablespoons flour
2 cups chicken broth
2 cups dairy sour cream
3 tablespoons paprika

1. Cook cabbage leaves 4 minutes in boiling salted water to cover. Drain and pat dry.
2. Mix chicken, onion, celery, mushrooms, garlic, salt, and thyme; stir in egg.
3. Place ½ cup of the chicken mixture in the center of each cabbage leaf. Fold sides of the cabbage leaf toward center, over filling, and then fold and overlap ends to make a small bundle. Fasten with wooden picks. Place in a 3-quart baking dish.
4. Heat butter in a large skillet. Blend in flour and heat until bubbly. Add chicken broth gradually, stirring until smooth. Blend in sour cream and paprika. Cook over low heat, stirring constantly, until thickened. Pour sauce over cabbage rolls. Cover baking dish.
5. Cook in a 350°F oven 35 minutes.

4 servings

Cauliflower Italiana

2 packages (10 ounces each) frozen
  cauliflower
2 tablespoons butter or margarine
½ clove garlic, minced
2 teaspoons flour
1 teaspoon salt
1 can (16 ounces) tomatoes
  (undrained)
1 small green pepper, coarsely
  chopped
¼ teaspoon oregano

1. Cook cauliflower following package directions; drain.
2. Meanwhile, heat butter with garlic in a saucepan. Stir in flour and salt and cook until bubbly.
3. Add tomatoes with liquid and bring to boiling, stirring constantly; cook 1 to 2 minutes. Stir in green pepper and oregano.
4. Pour hot sauce over cooked cauliflower.

About 6 servings

Corn Spoon Bread

1 quart milk
1 cup enriched yellow cornmeal
2 tablespoons finely chopped onion
2 tablespoons chopped parsley
4 eggs
2 tablespoons butter or margarine
2 tablespoons prepared baconlike
  pieces (a soy protein product)

1. Scald milk in top of a double boiler over simmering water.
2. Add cornmeal to scalded milk gradually, stirring constantly. Mix in onion and parsley. Cook over boiling water until thickened, about 10 minutes, stirring frequently and vigorously.
3. Meanwhile, beat eggs in a large bowl until thick and piled softly.
4. Remove double boiler top from water. Stir in butter and

2 teaspoons salt
1 teaspoon sugar
1 teaspoon baking powder
¼ teaspoon seasoned pepper
2 cups corn kernels (fresh, frozen, or canned)

baconlike pieces. Blend salt, sugar, baking powder, and seasoned pepper; stir into cornmeal mixture. Add hot mixture gradually to eggs, beating constantly. Mix in corn. Turn into a buttered 2-quart casserole.

5. Bake at 425°F 40 to 45 minutes, or until top is browned. Serve immediately.

6 to 8 servings

Ratatouille with Spanish Olives

1 medium eggplant (about 1½ pounds), pared and cut in 3 × ½-inch strips
2 zucchini, cut in ¼-inch slices
2 teaspoons salt
½ cup olive oil
2 onions, thinly sliced
2 green peppers, thinly sliced
2 cloves garlic, minced
3 tomatoes, peeled and cut in strips
1 cup sliced pimento-stuffed olives
¼ cup snipped parsley
¼ teaspoon ground pepper
Parsley, snipped

1. Toss eggplant and zucchini with 1 teaspoon salt and let stand 30 minutes. Drain and then dry on paper toweling.
2. Heat ¼ cup oil in a large skillet and lightly brown eggplant strips and then zucchini slices. Remove with slotted spoon; set aside.
3. Heat remaining oil in the skillet; cook onions and green peppers until tender. Stir in garlic. Put tomato strips on top; cover and cook 5 minutes. Gently stir in eggplant, zucchini, olives, ¼ cup parsley, remaining salt, and the pepper.
4. Simmer, covered, 20 minutes. Uncover and cook 5 minutes; baste with juices from bottom of skillet. Serve hot or cold, garnished with parsley.

6 to 8 servings

Fresh Corn Vinaigrette

4 ears fresh corn
¼ cup vegetable oil
2 tablespoons cider vinegar
¾ teaspoon lemon juice
1½ tablespoons chopped parsley
1 teaspoon salt
½ teaspoon sugar
¼ teaspoon basil
⅛ teaspoon cayenne pepper
1 large tomato, peeled and chopped
¼ cup chopped green pepper
¼ cup chopped green onion
Greens (optional)

1. Husk corn and remove silks. Fill a large kettle half full of water and bring to boiling. Add corn, cover, and return to boiling. Remove from heat and let stand 5 minutes. Drain and set aside to cool.
2. Mix oil, vinegar, lemon juice, parsley, salt, sugar, basil, and cayenne in a large bowl.
3. Cut corn off cob and add to bowl along with tomato, green pepper, and green onion; mix well. Cover and chill several hours.
4. Drain and serve on greens, if desired.

4 to 6 servings

Note: If desired, substitute 1½ cups (12-ounce can, drained, or 10-ounce package frozen, defrosted) whole kernel corn.

Fresh Peas with Basil

2 tablespoons butter or margarine
½ cup sliced green onions with tops
1½ cups shelled fresh peas (1½ pounds)
½ teaspoon sugar
½ teaspoon salt
⅛ teaspoon ground black pepper
¼ teaspoon basil
1 tablespoon snipped parsley
½ cup water

1. Heat butter in a skillet. Add green onions and cook 5 minutes, stirring occasionally. Add peas, sugar, salt, pepper, basil, parsley, and water.
2. Cook, covered, over medium heat 10 minutes, or until peas are tender.

About 4 servings

Note: If desired, use 1 package (10 ounces) frozen green peas and decrease water to ¼ cup.

Parsley-Buttered New Potatoes

18 small new potatoes
Boiling water
1½ teaspoons salt
2 tablespoons butter
1 tablespoon snipped parsley

Scrub potatoes and put into a saucepan. Pour in boiling water to a 1-inch depth. Add salt; cover and cook about 15 minutes, or until tender. Drain and peel. Return potatoes to saucepan and toss with butter and parsley.

About 6 servings

Note: Snipped chives, grated lemon peel, and lemon juice may be used instead of parsley.

Hash Brown Potatoes au Gratin

1 package (2 pounds) frozen chopped hash brown potatoes, partially defrosted
1½ teaspoons salt
Few grains pepper
¼ cup coarsely chopped green pepper
1 jar (2 ounces) sliced pimentos, drained and chopped
2 cups milk
¾ cup fine dry enriched bread crumbs
⅓ cup soft butter
⅔ cup shredded pasteurized process sharp American cheese

1. Turn potatoes into a buttered shallow 2-quart baking dish, separating into pieces. Sprinkle with salt and pepper. Add green pepper and pimentos; mix lightly. Pour milk over potatoes. Cover with aluminum foil.
2. Cook in a 350°F oven 1¼ hours, or until potatoes are fork-tender. Remove foil; stir potatoes gently. Mix bread crumbs, butter, and cheese. Spoon over top of potatoes. Return to oven and heat 15 minutes, or until cheese is melted.

About 6 servings

Potato Pancakes

Butter or margarine (enough, melted, for a ¼-inch layer)
2 tablespoons flour
1½ teaspoons salt
¼ teaspoon baking powder
⅛ teaspoon ground black pepper
6 medium potatoes, washed
2 eggs, well beaten

1. Heat butter in a heavy skillet over low heat.
2. Combine flour, salt, baking powder, and pepper and set aside.
3. Pare and finely grate potatoes; set aside.
4. Combine flour mixture with eggs and onion.
5. Drain liquid from grated potatoes; add potatoes to egg mixture and beat thoroughly.
6. When butter is hot, spoon batter into skillet, allowing

1 teaspoon grated onion
  Applesauce or maple syrup,
  warmed

about 2 tablespoonfuls for each pancake and leaving about 1 inch between cakes. Cook over medium heat until golden brown and crisp on one side. Turn carefully and brown on other side. Drain on absorbent paper. Serve with applesauce or maple syrup.

About 20 pancakes

Lacy French-Fried Onion Rings

1 cup enriched all-purpose flour
1 teaspoon baking powder
¼ teaspoon salt
1 egg, well beaten
1 cup milk
1 tablespoon vegetable oil
4 sweet Spanish onions
  Fat for deep frying heated to 375°F
  Salt or garlic salt

1. Blend flour, baking powder, and salt.
2. Combine egg, milk, and oil in a bowl and beat until thoroughly blended. Beat in the dry ingredients until batter is smooth. Cover.
3. Cut off root ends of onions; slip off the loose skins. Slice onions ¼ inch thick and separate into rings.
4. Using a long-handled two-tined fork, immerse a few onion rings at a time into the batter, lift out and drain over bowl a few seconds before dropping into heated fat. Turn only once as they brown; do not crowd.
5. When rings are golden brown on both sides, lift out and drain on absorbent paper-lined cookie sheet. Sprinkle with salt and serve hot.

About 6 servings

Lacy Cornmeal Onion Rings: Follow recipe for Lacy French-Fried Onion Rings. Substitute ½ **cup enriched cornmeal** for ⅔ cup flour.

To Freeze French-Fried Onions: Leaving the crisp, tender rings on the absorbent paper-lined cookie sheet on which they were drained, place in freezer and freeze quickly. Then carefully remove rings to moisture-vaporproof containers with layers of absorbent paper between each layer of onions; the rings may overlap some. Cover tightly, label, and freeze.

To Reheat Frozen French-Fried Onions: Removing the desired number of onion rings, arrange them (frozen) in a single layer on a cookie sheet. Heat in a 375°F oven several minutes, or until rings are crisp and hot.

Turnip Custard

2 pounds turnips
1 egg, well beaten
¼ cup finely crushed soda crackers
⅔ cup (6-ounce can) undiluted
  evaporated milk
1 teaspoon salt
  Few grains black pepper
1 cup (about 4 ounces) shredded
  sharp Cheddar cheese

1. Wash, pare, and cut turnips into pieces. Cook, uncovered, in boiling water to cover until turnips are tender, 15 to 20 minutes; drain. Mash and, if necessary, again drain turnips (about 2 cups mashed turnips).
2. Blend mashed turnips, egg, cracker crumbs, evaporated milk, salt, and pepper. Turn mixture into a buttered 1¼-quart baking dish. Set dish in a pan and pour in boiling water to a 1-inch depth.
3. Bake at 350°F 15 minutes. Sprinkle cheese over top. Bake 5 minutes, or until a knife inserted halfway between center and edge comes out clean. Remove from water immediately.

About 6 servings

Cracked-Wheat-Stuffed Tomatoes

½ cup cracked wheat or bulgur
1½ cups hot water
6 firm medium tomatoes, rinsed
⅛ teaspoon *each* sugar, salt, and pepper
3 tablespoons crushed dried mint
3 tablespoons warm water
1 small ripe avocado
1½ teaspoons salt
½ teaspoon sugar
2 tablespoons lemon juice
⅓ cup olive oil
¼ cup finely chopped green onion
¼ cup snipped parsley

1. Combine cracked wheat and hot water; set aside 30 minutes. Drain cracked wheat thoroughly and set aside.
2. Peel tomatoes. Cut off and discard a ½-inch slice from the top of each. Seed tomatoes. Scoop out pulp, chop it, and turn into a sieve to drain. Invert tomatoes on absorbent paper to drain 30 minutes. Mix ⅛ teaspoon sugar, ⅛ teaspoon salt, and pepper; sprinkle over pulp and insides of tomatoes.
3. Combine dried mint and warm water; set aside 15 minutes. Squeeze dry.
4. Peel avocado; put pulp into a bowl and mash with a fork. Beat in 1½ teaspoons salt, ½ teaspoon sugar, and lemon juice. Add oil in a thin stream, beating constantly. Mix in drained cracked wheat, tomato pulp, mint, green onion, and parsley. Fill tomatoes. Chill.

6 servings

Spinach Gnocchi

1½ cups milk
1 tablespoon butter or margarine
¼ teaspoon salt
Few grains nutmeg
¼ cup farina
½ cup well-drained cooked chopped spinach
1 egg, well beaten
1 tablespoon chopped onion, lightly browned in 1 teaspoon butter or margarine
1½ cups (about 6 ounces) shredded Swiss cheese
2 eggs, well beaten
¾ cup milk
1 tablespoon flour
1 teaspoon salt
Few grains nutmeg

1. Combine milk, butter, salt, and few grains nutmeg in a saucepan. Bring to boiling and add farina gradually, stirring constantly. Cook over low heat until mixture thickens.
2. Stir in spinach, egg, cooked onion, and 1 cup cheese; blend well. Set aside to cool slightly.
3. Drop mixture by tablespoonfuls close together in a well-greased shallow 9-inch baking dish or casserole. Sprinkle remaining cheese over mounds.
4. For topping, combine eggs, milk, flour, salt, and few grains nutmeg, blending well. Pour over spinach mixture in baking dish.
5. Bake at 350°F 35 to 40 minutes, or until golden brown on top. Serve at once.

4 to 6 servings

Apple-Stuffed Acorn Squash

2 acorn squash
2 tart apples
1½ teaspoons grated fresh lemon peel
1 tablespoon fresh lemon juice
¼ cup butter or margarine, melted
⅓ cup firmly packed brown sugar
 Salt
 Cinnamon
 Apple and lemon slices for
  garnish (optional)

1. Cut squash into halves lengthwise and scoop out seedy centers. Place cut side down in baking dish and pour in boiling water to a ½-inch depth. Bake at 400°F 20 minutes.
2. Pare, core, and dice apples; mix with lemon peel and juice, 2 tablespoons butter, and brown sugar.
3. Invert squash halves and brush with remaining 2 tablespoons butter; sprinkle with salt and cinnamon.
4. Fill squash halves with apple mixture. Pour boiling water into dish to a ½-inch depth; cover and bake 30 minutes.
5. Before serving, spoon pan juices over squash. If desired, garnish with apple and lemon slices.

4 servings

Spinach-Bacon Soufflé

2 cups firmly packed, finely chopped fresh spinach (dry the leaves before chopping)
¼ cup finely chopped green onions with tops
½ pound sliced bacon, cooked, drained, and crumbled
3 tablespoons butter or margarine
¼ cup enriched all-purpose flour
½ teaspoon salt
¼ to ½ teaspoon thyme
1 cup milk
3 egg yolks, well beaten
4 egg whites
2 teaspoons shredded Parmesan cheese

1. Toss the spinach, green onions, and bacon together in a bowl; set aside.
2. Heat butter in a saucepan over low heat. Blend in flour, salt, and thyme. Stirring constantly, heat until bubbly. Add milk gradually, continuing to stir. Bring rapidly to boiling and boil 1 to 2 minutes, stirring constantly.
3. Remove from heat and blend spinach-bacon mixture into the sauce. Stir in the beaten egg yolks; set aside to cool.
4. Meanwhile, beat egg whites until rounded peaks are formed (peaks turn over slightly when beater is slowly lifted upright); do not overbeat.
5. Gently spread spinach-bacon mixture over the beaten egg whites. Carefully fold together until ingredients are just blended.
6. Turn mixture into an ungreased 2-quart soufflé dish (straight-sided casserole); sprinkle top with Parmesan cheese.
7. Bake at 350°F 40 minutes, or until a knife comes out clean when inserted halfway between center and edge of soufflé and top is lightly browned. Serve immediately.

6 servings

Spinach-Cheese Bake

2 packages (10 ounces each) frozen chopped spinach
3 eggs, beaten
¼ cup enriched all-purpose flour
1 teaspoon seasoned salt
¼ teaspoon ground nutmeg
¼ teaspoon ground black pepper
2 cups (16 ounces) creamed cottage cheese
2 cups (8 ounces) shredded Swiss or Cheddar cheese

1. Cook spinach following package directions; drain.
2. Combine eggs, flour, seasoned salt, nutmeg, and pepper in a bowl. Mix in cottage cheese, Swiss cheese, and spinach.
3. Turn into a buttered 1½-quart casserole.
4. Bake at 325°F 50 to 60 minutes.

6 to 8 servings

Vegetable-Rice Medley

3 tablespoons butter or margarine
¾ cup chopped onion
1½ pounds zucchini, thinly sliced
1 can (16 ounces) whole kernel
   golden corn, drained
1 can (16 ounces) tomatoes
   (undrained)
3 cups cooked enriched white rice
1½ teaspoons salt
¼ teaspoon ground black pepper
¼ teaspoon ground coriander
¼ teaspoon oregano leaves

Heat butter in a large saucepan. Add onion and zucchini; cook until tender, stirring occasionally. Add corn, tomatoes with liquid, cooked rice, salt, pepper, coriander, and oregano; mix well. Cover and bring to boiling; reduce heat and simmer 15 minutes.

About 8 servings

Stuffed Baked Sweet Potatoes

4 medium sweet potatoes, washed
1 small ripe banana, peeled
2 tablespoons butter or margarine
⅓ cup fresh orange juice
1 tablespoon brown sugar
1½ teaspoons salt
¼ cup chopped pecans

1. Bake sweet potatoes at 375°F 45 minutes to 1 hour, or until tender when tested with a fork.
2. Cut a lengthwise slice from each potato. Scoop out sweet potatoes into a bowl; reserve shells. Mash banana with potatoes; add butter, orange juice, brown sugar, and salt and beat thoroughly. Spoon mixture into shells. Sprinkle with pecans. Set on a cookie sheet.
3. Return to oven 12 to 15 minutes, or until heated.

4 servings

Zucchini Boats

8 medium zucchini, washed and ends
   removed
1 medium tomato, cut in small pieces
¼ cup chopped salted almonds
1 tablespoon chopped parsley
1 teaspoon finely chopped onion
½ teaspoon seasoned salt
2 teaspoons butter, melted
¼ cup cracker crumbs

1. Cook zucchini in boiling salted water until crisp-tender, 7 to 10 minutes. Drain; cool.
2. Cut zucchini lengthwise into halves; scoop out and discard centers. Chop 2 shells coarsely; set remaining shells aside. Put chopped zucchini and tomato into a bowl. Add almonds, parsley, onion, and seasoned salt; mix well.
3. Spoon filling into zucchini shells. Mix butter and cracker crumbs. Sprinkle over filling. Set on a cookie sheet.
4. Place under broiler 4 inches from heat. Broil 3 minutes, or until crumbs are golden.

6 servings

Salads

An attractively arranged bowl of greens or a glistening molded salad can be a real eye-catcher on the dinner table. Salads can be an appetizing first course, an accompaniment to the entrée, or the main dish itself.

A tossed salad complements practically any meal, and using a variety of greens will give the salad its special character. Vegetables of all kinds make cool, tempting salads. Select a dressing that enhances but doesn't overpower the flavor and freshness of the salad. You'll find in this section a variety of recipes for all sorts of delicious make-at-home salad dressings.

Salads also play an important nutritional role in the diet. The fruits and vegetables used in salads are storehouses of essential vitamins and minerals. Macaroni, rice, and meat salads also provide protein, iron, and B vitamins.

Gourmet Potato Salad

5 cups cubed cooked potatoes
½ teaspoon salt
⅛ teaspoon ground black pepper
4 hard-cooked eggs, chopped
1 cup chopped celery
⅔ cup sliced green onions with tops
¼ cup chopped green pepper
1 cup large curd cottage cheese
¼ teaspoon dry mustard
½ teaspoon salt
    Few grains black pepper
⅔ cup (6-ounce can) undiluted
    evaporated milk
½ cup crumbled blue cheese
2 tablespoons cider vinegar
    Lettuce

1. Put potatoes into a large bowl and sprinkle with salt and pepper. Add eggs, celery, onions, and green pepper; toss lightly.
2. Put cottage cheese, dry mustard, salt, pepper, evaporated milk, blue cheese, and vinegar into an electric blender container. Blend thoroughly.
3. Pour dressing over mixture in bowl and toss lightly and thoroughly. Chill before serving to blend flavors.
4. Spoon chilled salad into a bowl lined with lettuce. Garnish as desired.

About 8 servings

Farmer's Chop Suey

1 large firm cucumber, pared and
    cut in small cubes
1 cup sliced red radishes
6 green onions with tops, sliced
3 firm ripe tomatoes, cut in chunks
½ teaspoon salt
⅛ teaspoon ground black pepper
1 to 1½ cups dairy sour cream

1. Put cucumber, radishes, green onions, and tomatoes into a large salad bowl. Sprinkle with salt and pepper; toss lightly.
2. Stir sour cream and spoon over all. Serve immediately.

About 6 servings

Broccoli Vinaigrette with Avocado

1 package (10 ounces) frozen broccoli
    spears
2 tablespoons olive oil
1 tablespoon tarragon vinegar
⅛ teaspoon salt
    Few grains pepper
¼ bunch watercress
1 medium ripe avocado
1 tablespoon chopped chives
    (optional)

1. Cook broccoli following package directions.
2. Combine oil, vinegar, salt, and pepper. Put broccoli into a bowl and pour dressing over it. Chill until ready to serve.
3. Arrange watercress on serving plate or individual salad plates.
4. Peel and slice avocado; arrange on watercress with broccoli. Sprinkle with chives, if desired. Drizzle remaining dressing over salad.

4 servings

Sauerkraut Slaw

2 cups (16-ounce can) sauerkraut,
    drained and snipped with
    scissors
1 onion, chopped (about ½ cup)
1 green pepper, sliced (about ¾ cup)
1 unpared red apple, diced (about 1
    cup)
⅓ to ½ cup sugar
1 can (16 ounces) sliced tomatoes or
    tomato wedges, drained
    Seasoned pepper

1. Combine sauerkraut, onion, green pepper, apple, and sugar in a serving bowl; toss until well mixed. Cover and refrigerate.
2. Before serving, overlap tomato slices around edge of bowl. Sprinkle slices with seasoned pepper.

8 to 12 servings

Stuffed Eggplant Salad

2 large eggplants
4 medium tomatoes, peeled and
    diced
⅓ cup thinly sliced green onion
⅓ cup olive or salad oil
½ cup fresh lemon juice
¼ cup chopped parsley
1 tablespoon sugar
2½ teaspoons salt
2 teaspoons oregano
¼ teaspoon ground black pepper

1. Wash and dry eggplants; place on a cookie sheet. Bake in a 375°F oven 35 to 45 minutes, or until tender when pierced with a fork. Cool.
2. Cut a thin lengthwise slice from the side of each eggplant; carefully spoon out pulp. Chill shells.
3. Dice pulp and put into a bowl. Add tomatoes, green onion, oil, lemon juice, parsley, sugar, salt, oregano, and pepper; toss to mix. Chill.
4. Before serving, drain off excess liquid from salad mixture. Spoon salad into shells.

6 servings

Bacon-Bean Salad

⅔ cup cider vinegar
¾ cup sugar
1 teaspoon salt
1 can (16 ounces) cut green beans
1 can (16 ounces) cut wax beans
1 can (16 ounces) kidney beans, thoroughly rinsed and drained
1 medium onion, quartered and finely sliced
1 medium green pepper, chopped
½ teaspoon freshly ground black pepper
⅓ cup salad oil
1 pound bacon, cut in 1-inch squares
Lettuce (optional)

1. Blend vinegar, sugar, and salt in a small saucepan. Heat until the sugar is dissolved and set aside.
2. Drain all beans and toss with onion, green pepper, vinegar mixture, and ground pepper. Pour oil over all and toss to coat evenly. Store in a covered container in refrigerator.
3. When ready to serve, fry bacon until crisp; drain on absorbent paper. Toss the bacon with bean mixture. If desired, serve the salad on crisp lettuce.

About 12 servings

Note: If desired, omit bacon.

Mixed Vegetable Salad

1 cup diced cooked potatoes
1½ cups cooked sliced carrots
1½ cups cooked whole or cut green beans (fresh, frozen, or canned)
1½ cups cooked green peas (fresh, frozen, or canned)
1 cup sliced or diced cooked beets
Bottled Italian-style salad dressing
Lettuce
1 cup sliced celery
1 small onion, chopped
2 hard-cooked eggs, chopped
¾ cup small pimento-stuffed olives
¾ cup mayonnaise
¼ cup chili sauce
1 teaspoon lemon juice

1. Put potatoes, carrots, beans, peas, and beets into separate bowls. Pour salad dressing over each vegetable; chill thoroughly.
2. To serve, drain vegetables and arrange in a lettuce-lined salad bowl along with celery, onion, eggs, and olives.
3. Blend mayonnaise, chili sauce, and lemon juice. Pass with the salad.

About 8 servings

Beef Salad Acapulco

3 cups cooked beef strips
¾ cup salad oil
½ cup red wine vinegar
1½ teaspoons salt
¼ teaspoon ground pepper
⅛ teaspoon cayenne pepper
1 tablespoon chili powder
Salad greens
Avocado slices, brushed with marinade
Onion and green pepper rings
Tomato wedges
Ripe olives

1. Put beef strips into a shallow dish. Combine oil, vinegar, salt, pepper, cayenne pepper, and chili powder in a bottle; cover and shake vigorously. Pour over beef strips. Cover; marinate several hours or overnight.
2. Remove beef from marinade and arrange on crisp greens on chilled salad plates. Garnish with avocado slices, onion rings, green pepper rings, tomato wedges, and ripe olives. Serve the marinade as the dressing.

4 to 6 servings

Greek-Style Lamb-and-Olive Salad

Greek-Style Salad Dressing:
- ½ cup olive or salad oil
- 1 cup red wine vinegar
- 3 to 4 tablespoons honey
- 1½ teaspoons salt
- ⅛ teaspoon dry mustard
- 2 teaspoons crushed dried mint leaves
- ¼ teaspoon crushed oregano
- ¼ teaspoon crushed thyme
- ¼ teaspoon anise seed

Salad:
- 1½ pounds roast lamb, trimmed of fat and cut in strips
- Curly endive
- 1 large cucumber, pared and sliced
- 4 medium tomatoes, sliced and quartered
- 1 cup pitted ripe olives

1. For dressing, mix oil, vinegar, honey, salt, dry mustard, mint, oregano, thyme, and anise.

2. Pour the dressing over cooked lamb in a bowl, cover, and marinate in refrigerator at least 1 hour, or until thoroughly chilled.

3. To serve, arrange curly endive in a large salad bowl. Toss cucumber, tomatoes, and olives with some of the dressing and turn into salad bowl. Spoon meat over vegetables and pour more dressing over all.

6 servings

Molded Spinach Cottage Cheese on Platter

- 1 package (10 ounces) frozen chopped spinach
- 2 envelopes unflavored gelatin
- ¾ cup water
- 2 chicken bouillon cubes
- 2 tablespoons lemon juice
- 1½ cups creamed cottage cheese
- ½ cup dairy sour cream
- ½ cup sliced celery
- ⅓ cup chopped green pepper
- 2 tablespoons minced green onion

1. Cook and drain spinach, reserving liquid. Add enough water to liquid to make ½ cup. Set spinach and liquid aside.

2. Soften gelatin in ¾ cup water in a saucepan; add bouillon cubes. Set over low heat; stirring occasionally, until gelatin and bouillon cubes are dissolved. Remove from heat; stir in spinach liquid and lemon juice. Set aside.

3. Beat cottage cheese until fairly smooth with mixer or in electric blender. Blend with sour cream and then gelatin mixture. Stir in spinach, celery, green pepper, and onion. Turn into a 5-cup mold. Chill until firm.

4. Unmold onto a chilled large platter. If desired, arrange slices of summer sausage around the mold.

6 to 8 servings

Chicken-Fruit Salad

- Creamy Cooked Salad Dressing (page 82)
- 3 cups cubed cooked chicken
- Bottled French dressing
- ½ cup diced celery
- 1 cup small seedless grapes
- ½ cup drained crushed pineapple; reserve syrup for dressing
- 1 orange, sectioned and sections cut in halves
- ½ cup toasted salted almonds, coarsely chopped
- 1 tablespoon minced crystallized ginger

1. Prepare Creamy Cooked Salad Dressing; refrigerate.

2. Toss chicken in a bowl with enough French dressing to coat thoroughly; cover and set in refrigerator to marinate about 3 hours, mixing occasionally.

3. Lightly toss together chicken, celery, grapes, pineapple, orange, almonds, and ginger. Pour desired amount of the dressing over chicken mixture and toss gently. Cover and chill thoroughly.

4. To serve, line a salad bowl with chilled crisp greens. Fill bowl with chicken salad.

About 8 servings

Garden-Green Salad Mold

1 package (3 ounces) lime-flavored
    gelatin
¼ teaspoon salt
1 cup boiling water
1 cup cold water
1 ripe medium avocado
1 tablespoon lemon juice
2 cups finely shredded cabbage
½ cup thinly sliced radishes
½ cup thinly sliced green onions with
    tops
    Crisp greens

1. Put gelatin and salt into a bowl; add boiling water and stir until completely dissolved. Blend in cold water. Chill until slightly thickened.
2. Mash avocado and stir in lemon juice; blend thoroughly with gelatin. Mix in cabbage, radishes, and green onions.
3. Turn into a 1-quart mold or individual molds and chill until firm. Unmold onto chilled serving plate and garnish with salad greens.

About 8 servings

Stewed Tomato Aspic

1 envelope unflavored gelatin
½ cup cold water
1 can (16 ounces) stewed tomatoes
1 tablespoon sugar
¼ teaspoon salt
1 tablespoon cider vinegar
1½ teaspoons prepared horseradish
1½ teaspoons grated onion
¼ teaspoon Worcestershire sauce
2 hard-cooked eggs, cut in quarters
    Salad greens

1. Sprinkle gelatin over water to soften.
2. Turn tomatoes into a saucepan and break up any large pieces with a spoon. Stir in sugar, salt, vinegar, horseradish, onion, and Worcestershire sauce and heat to boiling. Add softened gelatin and stir until dissolved.
3. Chill gelatin until slightly thickened.
4. Arrange egg quarters around bottom of a 3- or 4-cup mold. Spoon slightly thickened gelatin mixture into mold. Chill until firm.
5. Unmold and garnish with crisp greens.

4 to 6 servings

Rice Salad with Assorted Sausages

⅓ cup white wine vinegar
1 teaspoon lemon juice
¼ teaspoon French mustard
1 teaspoon salt
¼ teaspoon ground black pepper
⅓ cup salad oil
3 cups cooked enriched white rice,
    cooled
3 cups finely shredded red cabbage
½ cup raisins
½ cup walnut pieces
    Greens
    Link sausage (such as bratwurst,
    smoky links, and frankfurters),
    cooked

1. Put vinegar into a bottle. Add lemon juice, mustard, salt, and pepper. Cover and shake. Add oil and shake well.
2. Combine rice, cabbage, raisins, and walnuts in a bowl; chill.
3. When ready to serve, shake dressing well and pour over salad; toss until well mixed.
4. Arrange greens on luncheon plates, spoon salad on greens, and accompany with assorted sausages.

6 to 8 servings

Tossed Supper Salad

Dressing:
- 1 cup salad oil
- ½ cup cider vinegar
- 1 teaspoon salt
- 1 teaspoon sugar
- ½ teaspoon onion salt
- ¼ teaspoon crushed tarragon
- ¼ teaspoon paprika
- ¼ teaspoon dry mustard
- ¼ teaspoon celery salt
- ⅛ teaspoon garlic salt
- ⅛ teaspoon ground black pepper

Salad:
- 2 cans (6½ or 7 ounces each) tuna
- ½ head lettuce
- 1 cup spinach leaves, washed
- 1 cup diced celery
- ¾ cup chopped green pepper
- ½ cup cooked green peas
- 4 sweet pickles, chopped
- 4 radishes, thinly sliced
- 2 hard-cooked eggs, sliced
- 2 tablespoons chopped pimento
- 2 tomatoes, rinsed and cut in eighths
- 1 teaspoon salt
- Tomato wedges
- Ripe olives

1. For dressing, put oil and vinegar into a jar; mix salt, sugar, and seasonings; add to jar, cover, and shake well. Refrigerate until needed. Shake before using.
2. For salad, drain tuna well and separate into small chunks; put into a bowl. Toss tuna with ½ cup prepared dressing; cover and refrigerate 1 to 2 hours.
3. Tear lettuce and spinach into pieces and put into a large bowl. Add celery, green pepper, peas, pickles, radishes, eggs, and pimento; add the tuna with its dressing and tomatoes. Sprinkle with salt. Toss lightly until ingredients are mixed and lightly coated with dressing; add more dressing, if desired.
4. Garnish with tomato wedges and ripe olives.

8 to 10 servings

Note: Two cups of diced cooked chicken, turkey, veal, or pork may be substituted for tuna.

Hearty Bean Salad

- 1 can (15 ounces) kidney beans, drained
- 2 hard-cooked eggs, diced
- ¼ cup chopped onion
- ½ cup diced celery
- ⅓ cup drained sweet pickle relish
- ½ cup shredded sharp Cheddar cheese
- ½ cup dairy sour cream
- Lettuce

1. Mix kidney beans, eggs, onion, celery, relish, and cheese in a large bowl. Add sour cream and toss together lightly; chill.
2. Serve the salad on lettuce.

4 to 6 servings

Cinnamon Waldorf Molds

- ⅓ cup red cinnamon candies
- 3 cups water
- 2 packages (3 ounces each) cherry-flavored gelatin
- 1 tablespoon lemon juice

1. Heat cinnamon candies and water to boiling in a saucepan. Remove from heat and add gelatin and lemon juice; stir until gelatin and candies are dissolved.
2. Chill until slightly thickened.
3. Mix in celery, apples, marshmallows, and walnuts. Spoon

2 cups chopped celery
2 cups chopped unpared red apples
1 cup miniature marshmallows
½ cup chopped walnuts
Lettuce

into 6 to 8 individual fancy molds or turn into a 1½-quart mold. Chill until firm.
4. Unmold onto lettuce.

6 to 8 servings

Chef's Fruit Salad

Cinnamon-Buttered Raisins:
1 tablespoon butter or margarine, melted
½ cup dark raisins
½ cup golden raisins
½ teaspoon ground cinnamon

Salad:
Salad greens
1 quart shredded salad greens
6 cups mixed fruit
Creamy Lemon Celery-Seed Dressing or Celery-Seed Salad Dressing
1½ cups Swiss cheese strips
1½ cups cooked ham or turkey strips

1. For Cinnamon-Buttered Raisins, melt butter in a skillet. Mix in raisins and cinnamon. Set over low heat 5 minutes, stirring frequently. Cool.
2. Line a salad bowl with salad greens. Add shredded greens.
3. Arrange fruit in bowl. Spoon some of the desired dressing over all. Top with cheese and ham strips alternated with Cinnamon-Buttered Raisins. Serve with remaining dressing.

About 6 servings

Creamy Lemon Celery-Seed Dressing: Blend thoroughly **1½ cups mayonnaise, ¼ cup unsweetened pineapple juice, 1 teaspoon grated lemon peel, 1 tablespoon lemon juice, ½ teaspoon celery seed, and few drops Tabasco.** Cover and refrigerate at least 1 hour to blend flavors.

About 1½ cups dressing

Celery-Seed Salad Dressing: Combine in a small bowl **¼ cup sugar, ⅓ cup light corn syrup, ¼ cup cider vinegar, 1½ to 2 teaspoons celery seed, 1 teaspoon dry mustard, 1 teaspoon salt, few grains white pepper, and 1 teaspoon grated onion.** Beat with a rotary beater until mixture is thoroughly blended. Add **1 cup salad oil** very gradually, beating constantly. Continue beating until mixture thickens. Cover and chill thoroughly. Shake before serving.

2 cups dressing

Dubonnet Chicken Salad Mold

2 envelopes unflavored gelatin
1 cup cranberry juice cocktail
1 cup red Dubonnet
1 cup red currant syrup
1 envelope unflavored gelatin
¾ cup cold water
1 tablespoon soy sauce
1 cup mayonnaise
1½ cups finely diced cooked chicken
½ cup finely chopped celery
¼ cup toasted blanched almonds, finely chopped
½ cup whipping cream, whipped
Leaf lettuce
Cucumber slices, scored
Pitted ripe olives

1. Soften 2 envelopes gelatin in cranberry juice in a saucepan; set over low heat and stir until gelatin is dissolved. Remove from heat and stir in Dubonnet and currant syrup.
2. Pour into a 2-quart fancy tubed mold. Chill until set but not firm.
3. Meanwhile, soften 1 envelope gelatin in cold water in a saucepan. Set over low heat and stir until gelatin is dissolved.
4. Remove from heat and stir in soy sauce and mayonnaise until thoroughly blended. Chill until mixture becomes slightly thicker. Mix in chicken, celery, and almonds. Fold in whipped cream until blended.
5. Spoon mixture into mold over first layer. Chill 8 hours or overnight.
6. Unmold onto a chilled serving plate. Garnish with lettuce, cucumber, and olives.

About 10 servings

Shimmering Strawberry Mold

2 packages (3 ounces each)
    strawberry-flavored gelatin
1½ cups boiling water
2 bottles (7 ounces each) lemon-lime
    carbonated beverage
1 pint fresh ripe strawberries,
    rinsed and hulled
⅓ cup sugar
    Salad greens
    Whole strawberries (optional)

1. Turn gelatin into a bowl, add boiling water, and stir until completely dissolved. Mix in carbonated beverage. Stir frequently over ice and water until slightly thicker than consistency of thick unbeaten egg white.
2. Meanwhile, cut berries lengthwise into halves, if large; sprinkle with sugar and set aside.
3. Stir the berries into the slightly thickened gelatin. Spoon into a 2-quart fancy tubed mold (or 10 individual molds). Chill until firm.
4. Unmold onto a chilled serving plate; garnish with crisp salad greens and, if desired, strawberries.

About 10 servings

Note: If desired, nut-coated cream cheese balls may be added to the salad. Soften 1 package (8 ounces) cream cheese; shape into ½-inch balls and roll in finely chopped walnuts (about ¾ cup). Arrange 5 or 6 balls in bottom of 2-quart mold; spoon enough of the slightly thickened gelatin-strawberry mixture into mold to cover cheese balls. Continue layering with remaining balls and gelatin mixture. Chill until firm.

Wilted Cabbage

4 cups shredded cabbage
6 slices bacon
½ cup cider vinegar
¼ cup water
3 tablespoons sugar
½ teaspoon salt
¼ teaspoon dry mustard

1. Turn cabbage into a bowl.
2. Cook bacon until crisp in a skillet; drain, reserving ¼ cup drippings. Crumble bacon onto cabbage; set aside.
3. Put reserved drippings into skillet. Add vinegar, water, sugar, salt, and dry mustard. Heat to boiling, stirring to blend.
4. Pour dressing over cabbage and bacon; toss lightly to mix.

6 to 8 servings

Ham Mousse Piquant

2 packages (3 ounces each)
    lemon-flavored gelatin
¼ teaspoon salt
2 cups boiling water
1 cup cold water
¼ cup cider vinegar
2 teaspoons grated onion
¼ cup water
⅔ cup chopped sweet pickle
¼ cup diced pimento
⅔ cup mayonnaise or salad dressing
1 teaspoon Worcestershire sauce
1 cup chilled whipping cream,
    whipped
4 cups firmly packed coarsely ground
    cooked ham
1 cup sliced celery
    Watercress

1. Turn gelatin and salt into a bowl. Add boiling water and stir until gelatin is dissolved. Stir in cold water, vinegar, and onion.
2. Remove 2 cups of the mixture and stir in ¼ cup water; chill until mixture thickens slightly.
3. Mix pickle and pimento into the slightly thickened gelatin. Turn into a ring mold (11 to 12 cups). Chill until just set but not firm.
4. Meanwhile, chill remaining gelatin over ice and water, stirring frequently, until slightly thickened, then whip with rotary beater until fluffy.
5. Blend mayonnaise and Worcestershire sauce; fold into whipped cream. Combine whipped cream mixture, ham, celery, and whipped gelatin. Turn into mold over pickle layer. Chill until firm.
6. Unmold onto a chilled serving plate. Fill center of mold with watercress.

About 12 servings

Frosty Fruit Salad

1 cup chopped soft dried prunes
1 cup orange pieces (1 to 2 oranges)
1 can (13¼ ounces) pineapple tidbits,
    drained; reserve ¼ cup syrup
½ cup sliced maraschino cherries,
    well drained on absorbent paper
1 envelope unflavored gelatin
⅓ cup cold water
2 cups creamed cottage cheese
1 cup dairy sour cream
1 cup whipping cream, whipped
¾ cup sugar
¾ teaspoon salt
1 large ripe banana, sliced
½ cup chopped salted almonds

1. Prepare fruits and set aside.
2. Soften gelatin in cold water in a small saucepan. Set over low heat and stir until gelatin is dissolved.
3. Sieve cottage cheese into a bowl. Blend in reserved pineapple syrup, sour cream, whipped cream, sugar, and salt; stir in the dissolved gelatin. Add the reserved fruits, banana, and almonds; mix well. Turn into refrigerator trays and freeze.
4. Allow salad to soften slightly at room temperature before serving. To serve, cut into wedges.

About 12 servings

Vegetable Medley Salad Dressing Deluxe

1 cup salad oil
3 tablespoons cider vinegar
2 tablespoons prepared horseradish
1 tablespoon sugar
1 teaspoon dry mustard
1 teaspoon paprika
½ teaspoon seasoned salt
¾ teaspoon salt
⅛ teaspoon ground black pepper
Few grains cayenne pepper
1 medium ripe tomato, peeled and
    cut in pieces
1 small onion, peeled and cut in
    pieces
½ small cucumber, pared and cut in
    pieces
⅓ small ripe avocado, peeled and cut
    in pieces
1 large clove garlic, peeled

1. Put oil, vinegar, horseradish, sugar, seasonings, vegetables, avocado, and garlic into an electric blender container and blend thoroughly. Chill.
2. Serve on a tossed vegetable salad.

About 3½ cups dressing

Jiffy French Dressing

1 tablespoon sugar
1 teaspoon paprika
1 teaspoon dry mustard
1 teaspoon salt
⅛ teaspoon ground black pepper
1 cup salad oil
¼ cup vinegar or lemon juice

1. Blend sugar, paprika, dry mustard, salt, and pepper; put into a jar. Add oil and vinegar. Cover jar tightly and shake vigorously to blend. Store in refrigerator.
2. Before serving, shake dressing thoroughly.

1¼ cups dressing

Vegetable-Rice Medley, 72

Gourmet French Dressing

¾ cup olive oil
¼ cup vinegar (tarragon or cider)
¼ teaspoon Worcestershire sauce
1 clove garlic, cut in halves
1 teaspoon sugar
½ teaspoon salt
¼ teaspoon paprika
¼ teaspoon dry mustard
⅛ teaspoon ground black pepper
⅛ teaspoon ground thyme

1. Combine oil, vinegar, Worcestershire sauce, garlic, sugar, salt, paprika, dry mustard, pepper, and thyme in a jar; cover and shake well. Chill in refrigerator.
2. Before serving, remove garlic and beat or shake dressing thoroughly.

About 1 cup dressing

Roquefort French Dressing: Follow recipe for Gourmet French Dressing. Blend **3 ounces (about ¾ cup) Roquefort cheese,** crumbled, and **2 teaspoons water** until smooth. Add dressing slowly to cheese, blending well.

No-Oil Salad Dressing

½ cup water
½ cup white wine vinegar
1 tablespoon cold water
2 teaspoons cornstarch
1 tablespoon sugar
1 tablespoon chopped parsley
1 teaspoon salt
½ teaspoon basil
¼ teaspoon paprika
¼ teaspoon dry mustard
⅛ teaspoon ground white pepper

1. Heat ½ cup water and vinegar to boiling. Blend 1 tablespoon cold water and cornstarch; pour into vinegar mixture, stirring constantly.
2. Cook and stir until slightly thickened. Stir in sugar, parsley, salt, basil, paprika, dry mustard, and pepper. Chill thoroughly.
3. Serve on tossed salad greens.

About 1 cup dressing

Cooked Salad Dressing

¼ cup sugar
1 tablespoon flour
½ teaspoon dry mustard
½ teaspoon salt
⅛ teaspoon ground pepper
1 cup water
¼ cup cider vinegar
4 egg yolks, fork beaten
2 tablespoons butter or margarine

1. Blend sugar, flour, dry mustard, salt, and pepper in a heavy saucepan. Add water gradually, stirring constantly. Bring rapidly to boiling; cook and stir mixture 2 minutes. Stir in vinegar.
2. Stir about 3 tablespoons of the hot mixture into the beaten egg yolks. Immediately blend into mixture in saucepan. Cook and stir until slightly thickened.
3. Remove from heat and blend in butter. Cool; chill. Store in a covered jar in refrigerator.

About 1½ cups dressing

Creamy Cooked Salad Dressing

2 tablespoons sugar
⅛ teaspoon salt
2 tablespoons cider vinegar
2 tablespoons pineapple syrup
3 egg yolks, slightly beaten
1 tablespoon butter or margarine
1 cup chilled whipping cream, whipped

1. Mix sugar and salt in a heavy saucepan. Stir in vinegar and pineapple syrup. Bring to boiling, stirring constantly.
2. Stir about 2 tablespoons of the hot mixture into egg yolks until blended. Immediately blend into mixture in saucepan. Cook and stir until slightly thickened.
3. Remove from heat; blend in butter. Cool and chill.
4. Blend chilled mixture into whipped cream. Cover and refrigerate until ready to use.

About 2 cups dressing

Desserts

Nutritious eating does not mean giving up the pastries and sweets we all love. The fruits, milk products, eggs, and nuts in many delicious desserts are wholesome foods that belong in any healthful diet. Many desserts, such as fruit pies and cobblers, milk-based puddings, and ice cream, can count as a serving or portion of a serving from one of the Four Food Groups.

A dessert should not be just an afterthought to a meal, but rather it should complement it in terms of ingredients, color, flavor, and texture. Whatever the occasion, whether it's an everyday family meal, a company dinner, or a party, a homemade dessert will make it extra special.

Pie-Pan Apple Dessert

1 egg
¾ cup firmly packed brown sugar
½ cup enriched all-purpose flour
1 teaspoon baking powder
¼ teaspoon salt
¼ to ½ teaspoon ground nutmeg
1½ cups chopped pared apple
½ cup chopped pecans
   Lemon Sauce, whipped cream, or ice cream

1. Beat egg until light and fluffy. Beat in brown sugar. Mix flour, baking powder, salt, and nutmeg; add to egg mixture and blend.
2. Stir in apple and pecans. Spread in well-greased 8- or 9-inch pie pan or plate.
3. Bake at 350°F about 30 minutes, or until top is golden brown.
4. Serve warm with Lemon Sauce or desired topping.

About 6 servings

Lemon Sauce: Mix ⅓ cup sugar, 2 teaspoons cornstarch, and a few grains salt in a saucepan. Add 1 cup boiling water gradually, stirring constantly. Continue to stir and bring to boiling; simmer 5 minutes. Remove from heat. Blend in 2 tablespoons butter, ¾ teaspoon grated lemon peel, and 1½ tablespoons lemon juice. Serve warm.

Peaches 'n' Corn Bread, Shortcake Style

1 cup sifted enriched all-purpose
    flour
½ teaspoon baking soda
¼ teaspoon salt
1 cup enriched yellow cornmeal
¾ cup firmly packed light brown
    sugar
1 egg, beaten
½ cup buttermilk
⅓ cup dairy sour cream
    Peach Butter Elégante
    Sweetened fresh peach slices

1. Blend flour, baking soda, salt, cornmeal, and brown sugar in a bowl; set aside.
2. Beat egg, buttermilk, and sour cream until well blended; add to dry ingredients and stir until just smooth (do not overmix).
3. Turn into a greased 11×7×1½-inch pan and spread batter evenly.
4. Bake at 425°F about 20 minutes.
5. While still warm, cut corn bread into serving-size pieces, remove from pan, and split into two layers. Spread Peach Butter Elégante generously between layers. Top with peach slices.

9 or 12 servings

Peach Butter Elégante: Thaw **1 package (10 or 12 ounces) frozen sliced peaches.** Drain peaches and cut into pieces; set aside. Put **1 cup firm unsalted butter** or **1 cup margarine** into a small mixing bowl. Beat with electric mixer on high speed just until butter is whipped. Add **½ cup confectioners' sugar** gradually, beating thoroughly. Add the peaches, about 1 tablespoon at a time, beating thoroughly after each addition. (Do not allow butter to become too soft.) Chill until ready to use.

About 2 cups peach butter

Spicy Peach Cobbler

1 can (29 ounces) sliced peaches,
    drained; reserve 1 cup syrup
½ cup firmly packed brown sugar
2 tablespoons cornstarch
⅛ teaspoon salt
⅛ teaspoon ground cinnamon
⅛ teaspoon ground cloves
2 tablespoons cider vinegar
1 tablespoon butter or margarine
1 cup all-purpose biscuit mix
½ cup finely shredded sharp Cheddar
    cheese
2 tablespoons butter or margarine,
    melted
¼ cup milk

1. Put drained peaches into a shallow 1-quart baking dish. Set aside.
2. Mix brown sugar, cornstarch, salt, cinnamon, and cloves in a saucepan. Blend in reserved peach syrup and vinegar; add 1 tablespoon butter. Bring mixture to boiling, stirring frequently; cook until thickened, about 10 minutes. Pour over peaches and set in a 400°F oven.
3. Combine biscuit mix and cheese. Stir in melted butter and milk to form a soft dough. Remove dish from oven and drop dough by heaping tablespoonfuls on top of hot peaches.
4. Return to oven and bake 20 minutes, or until crust is golden brown. Serve warm.

6 servings

Cantaloupe Sherbet

2 cups ripe cantaloupe pieces
1 egg white
½ cup sugar
2 tablespoons fresh lime juice

1. Put melon pieces, egg white, sugar, and lime juice into an electric blender container. Cover and blend until smooth.
2. Turn into a shallow baking dish. Set in freezer; stir occasionally during freezing.
3. To serve, spoon into chilled dessert dishes.

About 1½ pints sherbet

Pineapple Sherbet: Follow recipe for Cantaloupe Sherbet; substitute **2 cups fresh pineapple pieces** for cantaloupe.

Watermelon Sherbet: Follow recipe for Cantaloupe Sherbet; substitute **2 cups watermelon pieces** for cantaloupe and, if desired, decrease sugar to ¼ cup.

Banana-Pineapple Ice Cream

2 cups mashed ripe bananas (about 5 medium)
1 cup sugar
1 teaspoon grated orange peel
1 teaspoon grated lemon peel
3 tablespoons lemon juice
2 tablespoons lime juice
1½ cups unsweetened pineapple juice
⅓ cup orange juice
2 cans (14½ ounces each) evaporated milk

1. Crushed ice and rock salt will be needed. Wash and scald cover, container, and dasher of a 3- or 4-quart ice cream freezer. Chill thoroughly.
2. Combine bananas, sugar, orange peel, lemon peel, lemon juice, and lime juice; blend thoroughly. Set aside about 10 minutes.
3. Stir fruit juices into banana mixture. Add evaporated milk gradually, stirring until well blended.
4. Fill chilled freezer container no more than two-thirds full with ice cream mixture. Cover tightly. Set into freezer tub. (For electric freezer, follow the directions.)
5. Fill tub with alternate layers of crushed ice and rock salt, using 8 parts ice to 1 part salt. Turn handle slowly 5 minutes. Then turn rapidly until handle becomes difficult to turn (about 15 minutes), adding ice and salt as necessary.
6. Wipe cover and remove dasher. Pack down ice cream and cover with waxed paper or plastic wrap. Replace lid. (Plug dasher opening unless freezer has a solid cover.) Repack freezer container in ice, using 4 parts ice to 1 part salt. Cover with heavy paper or cloth. Let ripen 2 hours.

About 2 quarts ice cream

Quick Applesauce Whip

1 can (16 ounces) applesauce
½ teaspoon grated lemon peel
2 teaspoons lemon juice
½ teaspoon ground cinnamon
3 egg whites
⅛ teaspoon salt
6 tablespoons sugar
Ground nutmeg

1. Combine applesauce, lemon peel, juice, and cinnamon.
2. Beat egg whites and salt until frothy. Add sugar gradually, beat well. Continue beating until rounded peaks are formed. Fold beaten egg whites into applesauce mixture.
3. Spoon immediately into dessert dishes. Sprinkle nutmeg over each serving.

About 6 servings

Bananas with Royal Pineapple Sauce

3 tablespoons dark brown sugar
2 teaspoons cornstarch
1 can (8¼ ounces) crushed pineapple (undrained)
1 tablespoon butter
⅛ teaspoon almond extract
¼ teaspoon grated lemon peel
1 tablespoon lemon juice
¼ cup butter
4 firm bananas, peeled
2 tablespoons flaked coconut

1. Mix sugar and cornstarch in a saucepan. Add pineapple with syrup, 1 tablespoon butter, and almond extract; mix well. Bring to boiling, stirring constantly until thickened.
2. Remove from heat and stir in lemon peel and juice. Set the sauce aside.
3. Heat ¼ cup butter in a heavy skillet. Add bananas; turn them by rolling to cook evenly and brown lightly. (Do not overcook or fruit will lose its shape.)
4. Allowing one-half banana per person, serve at once topped with the warm pineapple sauce. Sprinkle with coconut.

8 servings

Purple Plum Crunch

5 cups pitted, quartered fresh purple plums
¼ cup firmly packed brown sugar
3 tablespoons flour
½ teaspoon ground cinnamon
1 cup enriched all-purpose flour
1 cup sugar
1 teaspoon baking powder
¼ teaspoon salt
¼ teaspoon ground mace
1 egg, well beaten
½ cup butter or margarine, melted and cooled

1. Put plums into a shallow 2-quart baking dish or casserole.
2. Mix brown sugar, 3 tablespoons flour, and cinnamon; sprinkle over plums and mix gently with a fork.
3. Blend 1 cup flour, sugar, baking powder, salt, and mace thoroughly. Add to beaten egg and stir with a fork until mixture is crumbly. Sprinkle evenly over plums in baking dish. Pour melted butter evenly over the topping.
4. Bake at 375°F 40 to 45 minutes, or until topping is lightly browned. Serve warm.

6 to 8 servings

Note: Other fresh fruits may be substituted for the plums.

Chocolate Peanut Butter Pudding

1 small package chocolate pudding and pie filling (not instant)
1 can (14½ ounces) evaporated milk
⅔ cup water
⅓ cup peanut butter
Slightly sweetened whipped cream (optional)
Chopped salted peanuts (optional)

1. Empty pudding mix into a saucepan, then stir in evaporated milk and water.
2. Cook and stir over moderate heat until thickened, about 5 minutes. Remove from heat and stir in peanut butter. Cover and chill.
3. To serve, spoon into dessert dishes. If desired, top with whipped cream and peanuts.

4 to 6 servings

Steamed Pumpkin Pudding

Pudding:
1¼ cups fine dry bread crumbs
½ cup enriched all-purpose flour
1 cup firmly packed brown sugar
1 teaspoon baking powder
½ teaspoon baking soda
½ teaspoon salt
½ teaspoon ground cinnamon
½ teaspoon ground cloves
½ cup salad oil
½ cup undiluted evaporated milk
2 eggs
1½ cups canned pumpkin

Lemon Nut Sauce:
½ cup butter or margarine
2 cups confectioners' sugar
¼ teaspoon salt
¼ teaspoon ground ginger
¼ cup lemon juice
½ cup chopped walnuts

1. Blend bread crumbs, flour, brown sugar, baking powder, baking soda, salt, cinnamon, and cloves in a large bowl.
2. Beat oil, evaporated milk, eggs, and pumpkin. Add to dry ingredients; mix until well blended.
3. Turn into a well-greased 2-quart mold. Cover tightly with a greased cover, or tie greased aluminum foil tightly over mold. Place mold on trivet or rack in a steamer or deep kettle with a tight-fitting cover.
4. Pour in boiling water to no more than one half the height of the mold. Cover steamer, bring water to boiling, and keep boiling at all times. If necessary, add more boiling water during cooking period.
5. Steam the pudding 2½ to 3 hours, or until a wooden pick inserted in center comes out clean.
6. For Lemon Nut Sauce, beat butter in a bowl. Blend confectioners' sugar, salt, and ginger; add gradually to butter, beating well. Add lemon juice gradually, continuing to beat until blended. Mix in walnuts.
7. Remove pudding from steamer and unmold onto a serving plate. Serve pudding with Lemon Nut Sauce.

About 12 servings

Note: If pudding is to be stored and served later, unmold onto a rack and cool thoroughly. Wrap in aluminum foil or return to mold and store in a cool place. Before serving, resteam pudding about 3 hours, or until thoroughly heated.

Individual Fruit Puddings

Pudding:
2 medium oranges
1½ cups sifted enriched all-purpose flour
1 teaspoon baking soda
¼ teaspoon salt
¼ teaspoon ground cinnamon
¼ teaspoon ground cloves
¼ teaspoon ground nutmeg
¼ cup shortening
1 cup firmly packed brown sugar
1 egg, well beaten
1 cup dark seedless raisins
½ cup pitted dates, cut in pieces
½ cup walnuts, coarsely chopped

Orange Sauce:
¾ cup sugar
2 tablespoons cornstarch
⅛ teaspoon salt
¾ cup orange juice
½ cup water
1 teaspoon grated orange peel
1 tablespoon butter or margarine

1. For pudding, grease eight 5-ounce custard cups. Set aside.
2. Peel oranges; slice into cartwheels, and cut into pieces; reserve juice as it collects.
3. Blend flour, baking soda, salt, cinnamon, cloves, and nutmeg. Set aside.
4. Beat shortening; add brown sugar gradually, beating until fluffy. Add egg and beat thoroughly.
5. Mix in the orange pieces, reserved juice, raisins, dates, and walnuts. Blend in the dry ingredients.
6. Fill custard cups about two-thirds full with mixture; cover tightly with aluminum foil. Set in a pan and fill pan with water to a 1-inch depth. Cover pan with aluminum foil.
7. Cook in a 325°F oven 2 hours.
8. For Orange Sauce, mix sugar, cornstarch, and salt in a saucepan. Add orange juice and water gradually, stirring constantly. Bring to boiling, stirring constantly until thickened; cook over low heat 6 to 8 minutes, stirring occasionally.
9. Remove from heat. Blend in orange peel and butter. Keep warm.
10. Unmold puddings while hot onto dessert plates and spoon sauce over each.

8 servings

Blueberry-Orange Parfaits

2 tablespoons cornstarch
1 cup sugar
½ teaspoon salt
2 cups orange juice
2 eggs, beaten
½ teaspoon grated lemon peel
2 tablespoons sugar
2 cups fresh blueberries
Whipped cream (optional)

1. Mix cornstarch, 1 cup sugar, and salt in a heavy saucepan. Add a small amount of the orange juice and blend until smooth. Stir in remaining orange juice.
2. Bring mixture to boiling, stirring constantly, and cook 3 to 5 minutes.
3. Stir about 3 tablespoons of the hot mixture into beaten eggs; immediately blend with mixture in saucepan.
4. Cook and stir about 3 minutes. Remove from water and cool. Stir in lemon peel. Chill.
5. Meanwhile, sprinkle 2 tablespoons sugar over blueberries and allow to stand at least 30 minutes. Spoon alternating layers of custard and blueberries in parfait glasses, beginning with a layer of custard and ending with blueberries. Top with whipped cream, if desired.

6 servings

Ginger-Yam Mousse

1½ cups mashed cooked yams (about 3 medium yams)
1 cup sugar
2 teaspoons ground ginger
1 teaspoon ground nutmeg
½ teaspoon ground cinnamon
Few grains salt
3 egg yolks, fork beaten
2 cups milk
½ teaspoon grated lemon peel
½ teaspoon lemon juice
½ cup half-and-half
3 egg whites
¼ cup sugar
Whipped dessert topping
Toasted slivered almonds

1. Put mashed yams into a heavy saucepan. Blend 1 cup sugar, spices, and salt. Mix with yams, then mix in egg yolks and milk. Cook over medium heat, stirring constantly, until mixture is thick. Remove from heat when mixture just comes to boiling.
2. Cool, stirring occasionally. Blend in lemon peel, juice, and half-and-half.
3. Beat egg whites until frothy; add ¼ cup sugar gradually, continuing to beat until stiff peaks are formed. Fold into completely cooled yam mixture.
4. Turn into a 6½-cup ring mold, spreading evenly. Freeze until firm, about 3½ hours.
5. Allow mousse to soften slightly at room temperature before unmolding. Unmold onto a chilled plate. Spoon whipped dessert topping into center and sprinkle with almonds.

6 to 8 servings

Citrus Bundt Cake

¾ cup butter
2 teaspoons grated lemon peel
2 teaspoons grated orange peel
1¾ cups sugar
3 eggs
3⅓ cups sifted enriched all-purpose flour
1 tablespoon baking powder
½ teaspoon salt
1 cup milk
2 tablespoons lemon juice
2 tablespoons orange juice
⅓ cup sugar
Fruit sauce (optional)

1. Cream butter, grated peels, and 1¾ cups sugar until light and fluffy. Add eggs, one at a time, beating thoroughly after each addition.
2. Blend flour, baking powder, and salt. Mix into creamed mixture alternately with milk. Turn into a generously buttered 10-inch Bundt pan or angel food cake pan.
3. Bake at 325°F 60 to 75 minutes, or until a cake tester comes out clean. Remove from pan immediately and place on wire rack set over a shallow pan.
4. Combine fruit juices and ⅓ cup sugar in a small saucepan. Bring to boiling and boil 3 minutes. Drizzle over warm cake; cool completely before serving.
5. Slice and serve with a fruit sauce, if desired.

One 10-inch Bundt cake

Chocolate Pound Cake Loaf

3 cups sifted enriched all-purpose flour
2 teaspoons baking powder
¼ teaspoon salt
½ cup cocoa, sifted
1 cup butter or margarine
½ cup lard
1 tablespoon vanilla extract
½ teaspoon almond extract
3 cups sugar
1 cup eggs (5 or 6)
1¼ cups milk

1. Lightly grease (bottom only) two 9×5×3-inch loaf pans. Line bottoms with waxed paper; grease paper. Set aside.
2. Combine flour, baking powder, salt, and cocoa and blend thoroughly. Set aside.
3. Cream butter and lard with extracts in a large bowl. Add sugar gradually, creaming thoroughly after each addition. Add eggs, one at a time, beating until fluffy after each addition.
4. Beating only until blended after each addition, alternately add dry ingredients in fourths and milk in thirds to creamed mixture.
5. Turn equal amounts of batter into prepared loaf pans. Spread batter evenly. (Top of baked cakes may have a slight crack down center.) Place pans on center of oven rack so that top of batter will be at center of oven.
6. Bake at 325°F about 65 minutes, or until cake tester inserted in center comes out clean.
7. Cool cakes in pans 15 minutes on wire racks. Loosen sides with a spatula and turn onto rack. Peel off paper, turn right side up, and cool completely.

Two loaf cakes

Dutch Cocoa Loaf Cake: Follow directions for Chocolate Pound Cake Loaf except substitute ⅔ **cup Dutch process cocoa** for the ½ cup cocoa and increase butter or margarine to 1½ cups; omit lard.

Cranberry Upside-Down Cake

Topping:
¼ cup butter or margarine
⅔ cup sugar
1 tablespoon grated orange peel
½ teaspoon vanilla extract
2 cups fresh cranberries, washed and coarsely chopped
⅓ cup sugar

Cake:
1½ cups sifted enriched cake flour
2 teaspoons baking powder
½ teaspoon salt
½ cup butter or margarine
1 teaspoon vanilla extract
½ cup sugar
1 egg
½ cup milk

1. For topping, heat butter in a saucepan. Add ⅔ cup sugar, orange peel, and vanilla extract; blend thoroughly. Spread mixture evenly in an 8×8×2-inch pan.
2. Combine cranberries and ⅓ cup sugar. Spread over mixture in pan; set aside.
3. For cake, blend flour, baking powder, and salt; set aside.
4. Cream butter with vanilla extract. Add sugar gradually, creaming until fluffy after each addition. Add egg and beat thoroughly.
5. Beating only until smooth after each addition, alternately add dry ingredients in thirds and milk in halves to creamed mixture. Turn batter over cranberry mixture and spread evenly.
6. Bake at 350°F about 50 minutes.
7. Remove from oven and let stand 1 to 2 minutes in pan on wire rack. To remove from pan, run spatula gently around sides. Cover with a serving plate and invert; allow pan to remain over cake 1 or 2 minutes. Lift pan off. Serve cake warm or cool.

One 8-inch square cake

Date Spice Cake

2¼ cups sifted enriched all-purpose flour
  2 teaspoons baking powder
  ¼ teaspoon baking soda
  ½ teaspoon salt
  2 teaspoons ground nutmeg
  2 teaspoons ground ginger
  ⅔ cup shortening
  1 teaspoon grated orange peel
  1 teaspoon grated lemon peel
  1 cup sugar
  2 eggs
  1 cup buttermilk
  1 cup chopped dates

1. Grease a 9×9×2-inch pan. Line with waxed paper cut to fit bottom; grease paper. Set aside.
2. Blend flour, baking powder, baking soda, salt, nutmeg, and ginger.
3. Beat shortening with orange and lemon peels. Add sugar gradually, creaming until fluffy after each addition.
4. Add eggs, one at a time, beating thoroughly after each addition.
5. Beating only until smooth after each addition, alternately add dry ingredients in fourths and buttermilk in thirds to creamed mixture. Mix in dates. Turn batter into prepared pan.
6. Bake at 350°F about 45 minutes.
7. Remove from oven. Cool 5 to 10 minutes in pan on wire rack. Remove cake from pan and peel off paper; cool cake on rack.

One 9-inch square cake

Carrot Cupcakes

1½ cups sifted enriched all-purpose flour
  1 teaspoon baking powder
  1 teaspoon baking soda
  1 teaspoon ground cinnamon
  ½ teaspoon salt
  1 cup sugar
  ¾ cup vegetable oil
  2 eggs
  1 cup grated raw carrots
  ½ cup chopped nuts

1. Blend flour, baking powder, baking soda, cinnamon, and salt. Set aside.
2. Combine sugar and oil in a bowl and beat thoroughly. Add eggs, one at a time, beating thoroughly after each addition. Mix in carrots. Add dry ingredients gradually, beating until blended. Mix in nuts.
3. Spoon into paper-baking-cup-lined muffin-pan wells.
4. Bake at 350°F 15 to 20 minutes.

About 16 cupcakes

Triple-Treat Walnut Bars

  ½ cup butter or margarine
  1 package (3 ounces) cream cheese
  ½ cup firmly packed dark brown sugar
  1 cup whole wheat flour
  ⅓ cup toasted wheat germ
  1 package (6 ounces) semisweet chocolate pieces
  2 eggs
  ½ cup honey
  ⅓ cup whole wheat flour
  ⅓ cup instant nonfat dry milk
  ¼ teaspoon salt
  ¼ teaspoon ground cinnamon
  ¼ teaspoon ground mace
1½ cups chopped walnuts

1. Cream butter, cheese, and sugar in a bowl until light. Add 1 cup whole wheat flour and wheat germ and mix until smooth. Turn into a greased 13×9×2-inch pan; spread evenly.
2. Bake at 375°F 15 to 18 minutes, until edges are very lightly browned and top is firm.
3. Remove from oven and sprinkle with chocolate. Let stand about 5 minutes, or until chocolate softens, then spread it evenly over baked layer.
4. Combine eggs and honey; beat just until well blended. Add ⅓ cup whole wheat flour, dry milk, salt, cinnamon, mace, and walnuts; mix well. Spoon over the chocolate.
5. Return to oven and bake 18 to 20 minutes, or until top is set. Cool in pan, then cut into bars or diamonds.

About 3 dozen cookies

Swiss Chocolate Squares

Cake:
- 1 cup water
- ½ cup soft margarine
- 1½ ounces (1½ squares) unsweetened chocolate
- 2 cups enriched all-purpose flour
- 2 cups sugar
- 2 eggs
- ½ cup dairy sour cream
- 1 teaspoon baking soda
- ¼ teaspoon salt

Milk Chocolate Frosting:
- ½ cup soft margarine
- 6 tablespoons milk
- 1½ ounces (1½ squares) unsweetened chocolate
- 4½ cups confectioners' sugar
- 1 teaspoon vanilla extract
- ½ cup chopped nuts

1. For cake, combine water, margarine, and chocolate in a saucepan. Set over medium heat and bring to boiling, stirring occasionally. Remove from heat.

2. Blend flour and sugar; stir into the cooked chocolate mixture. Beat in eggs and sour cream. Blend baking soda and salt; beat in. Turn into a greased 15×10×1-inch jelly-roll pan and spread evenly.

3. Bake at 375°F 20 to 25 minutes. Cool on a wire rack.

4. For Milk Chocolate Frosting, combine margarine, milk, and chocolate in a saucepan. Set over medium heat and bring to boiling; boil 1 minute, stirring constantly. Remove from heat.

5. Stir in confectioners' sugar, adding gradually, and beat until smooth. Stir in vanilla extract.

6. Turn frosting onto warm cake and spread evenly. Sprinkle with nuts. Cool completely before cutting into squares.

1½ to 3 dozen cake squares

Choco-Raisin Candy

- ¾ cup dark seedless raisins
- ½ cup canned chocolate frosting
  Finely chopped nuts, flaked coconut, cocoa, or equal parts confectioners' sugar and cocoa

Mix raisins and chocolate frosting. Chill thoroughly. Working quickly, form mixture into 1-inch balls and coat as desired. Refrigerate before serving.

1½ dozen candy balls

Peanut Butter Fudge

- 1 cup undiluted evaporated milk
- 2 cups sugar
- ¼ cup butter or margarine
- 1 cup miniature marshmallows
- 1 jar (12 ounces) crunchy peanut butter
- 1 teaspoon vanilla extract

1. Combine evaporated milk, sugar, and butter in a heavy 10-inch skillet. Set over medium heat, bring to boiling, and boil 4 minutes, stirring constantly.

2. Remove from heat and stir in marshmallows, peanut butter, and vanilla extract until evenly blended.

3. Turn into a buttered 8-inch square pan and spread to corners. Chill before cutting into squares.

About 2 pounds fudge

Note: This fudge may be prepared in an electric skillet. Set temperature at 280°F, bring mixture to boiling, and boil about 5 minutes.

Spicy Walnut Diamonds

2½ cups sifted all-purpose flour
2 tablespoons cocoa
1½ teaspoons baking powder
1 teaspoon salt
½ teaspoon ground nutmeg
¼ teaspoon ground cloves
2 cups firmly packed brown sugar
3 eggs
½ cup honey
½ cup butter or margarine, melted
1½ cups chopped walnuts (1 cup
      medium and ½ cup fine)
½ cup confectioners' sugar
2 to 3 teaspoons milk

1. Blend flour, cocoa, baking powder, salt, nutmeg, and cloves.
2. Combine brown sugar and eggs in a large bowl; beat until well blended and light. Add honey, butter, and flour mixture and mix until smooth.
3. Stir in the 1 cup medium walnuts, and spread evenly in a greased 15×10×1-inch jelly-roll pan. Sprinkle the ½ cup fine walnuts over top.
4. Bake at 375°F about 20 minutes, or just until top springs back when touched lightly in center. Cool in pan.
5. Mix confectioners' sugar and enough milk to make a smooth, thin glaze. Spread over cooled layer. Cut into diamonds or bars.

About 4 dozen cookies

Tropichocolate Wafers

1½ cups sifted enriched all-purpose
      flour
½ teaspoon baking soda
½ teaspoon salt
½ cup cocoa
½ cup butter or margarine
½ teaspoon vanilla extract
1 cup firmly packed brown sugar
1 egg
¾ cup flaked coconut

1. Blend flour, baking soda, salt, and cocoa. Set aside.
2. Cream butter with vanilla extract. Add brown sugar gradually, creaming until fluffy. Add egg and beat thoroughly.
3. Mixing until well blended after each addition, add dry ingredients in thirds to creamed mixture. Stir in coconut.
4. Chill dough in refrigerator until easy to handle, then shape into 2 rolls about 1½ inches in diameter. Wrap each roll in waxed paper, aluminum foil, or plastic wrap. Chill several hours or overnight.
5. Remove rolls of dough from refrigerator as needed. Cut dough into ⅛-inch slices. Place slices about 1½ inches apart on lightly greased cookie sheets.
6. Bake at 400°F 5 to 8 minutes. Cool cookies on wire racks.

About 5 dozen cookies

Butterscotchies

½ cup undiluted evaporated milk
¾ cup sugar
¼ teaspoon salt
2 tablespoons butter or margarine
1 package (6 ounces)
      butterscotch-flavored pieces
1 teaspoon vanilla extract
1 cup flaked coconut
½ cup coarsely chopped walnuts
2 to 2½ cups crisp enriched
      ready-to-eat cereal

1. Put evaporated milk, sugar, salt, and butter into a heavy 2-quart saucepan. Bring to a full boil, stirring constantly, and boil 2 minutes.
2. Remove from heat. Add butterscotch pieces and vanilla extract; stir until smooth. Add coconut, walnuts, and cereal; toss lightly until well coated.
3. Drop by rounded teaspoonfuls onto a cookie sheet lined with waxed paper or aluminum foil. Allow to stand until set.

About 1½ pounds candy

Peanut Blonde Brownies

½ cup chunk-style peanut butter
¼ cup butter or margarine
1 teaspoon vanilla extract
1 cup firmly packed light brown
  sugar
2 eggs
½ cup enriched all-purpose flour
1 cup chopped salted peanuts
  Confectioners' sugar

1. Cream peanut butter, butter, and vanilla extract in a bowl. Add brown sugar gradually, beating well after each addition.
2. Add eggs, one at a time, beating thoroughly after each addition until creamy.
3. Add flour in halves, beating until blended after each addition. Stir in peanuts. Turn mixture into a greased 8×8×2-inch pan and spread evenly.
4. Bake at 350°F 30 to 35 minutes.
5. Remove from oven and cool in pan 5 minutes. Cut into 2-inch squares. Remove from pan and cool on a wire rack. Sift confectioners' sugar over tops.

16 brownies

Pineapple Volcano Chiffon Pie

2 envelopes unflavored gelatin
½ cup sugar
¼ teaspoon salt
3 egg yolks, fork beaten
½ cup water
1 can (20 ounces) crushed pineapple
  (undrained)
¼ teaspoon grated lemon peel
1 tablespoon lemon juice
3 egg whites
  Frozen dessert topping, thawed, or
    whipped dessert topping
1 baked 9-inch graham cracker crust
1 can (8¼ ounces) crushed pineapple,
  drained

1. Mix gelatin, ¼ cup sugar, and salt in the top of a double boiler.
2. Beat egg yolks and water together. Stir into gelatin mixture along with undrained pineapple.
3. Set over boiling water. Thoroughly beat mixture and continue cooking 5 minutes to cook egg yolks and dissolve gelatin, stirring constantly.
4. Remove from water; mix in lemon peel and juice. Chill, stirring occasionally until mixture mounds slightly when dropped from a spoon.
5. Beat egg whites until frothy. Gradually add remaining ¼ cup sugar, beating until stiff peaks are formed. Fold into gelatin mixture.
6. Turn filling into crust; chill.
7. Garnish pie with generous mounds of the dessert topping. Spoon on remaining crushed pineapple to resemble "volcanoes."

One 9-inch pie

Cherry-Rhubarb Pie

1 can (16 ounces) pitted tart red
  cherries (water packed),
  drained
1 pound fresh rhubarb, sliced about
  ⅛ inch thick
1¼ cups sugar
¼ cup quick-cooking tapioca
⅛ teaspoon baking soda
½ teaspoon almond extract
  Few drops red food coloring
  Pastry for a 2-crust 9-inch pie

1. Mix cherries, rhubarb, sugar, tapioca, baking soda, almond extract, and red food coloring; let stand 20 minutes.
2. Prepare pastry. Roll out enough pastry to line a 9-inch pie pan or plate; line pie pan. Roll out remaining pastry for top crust and slit pastry with knife in several places to allow steam to escape during baking.
3. Pour filling into pastry-lined pan; cover with top crust and flute edge.
4. Bake at 450°F 10 minutes. Turn oven control to 350°F and bake 40 to 45 minutes. Remove from oven and set on a wire rack. Serve warm or cooled.

One 9-inch pie

Index